CHILDREN'S
PLAY

CHILDREN'S PLAY

EILEEN FURSLAND
CONSULTANT: SARAH CROMBIE, MCSP,SRP

 © 1989 Great Ormond Street Hospital Children's Charity

First published in 1998 by Virgin Books,
an imprint of Virgin Publishing Ltd
332 Ladbroke Grove, London W10 5AH

ISBN: 1 85227 741 6

Printed and bound by
All special photography by J. Catt
Clothes and props courtesy of Early Learning Centre
Designed by Slatter~Anderson
For Virgin Publishing: Carolyn Price

Contents

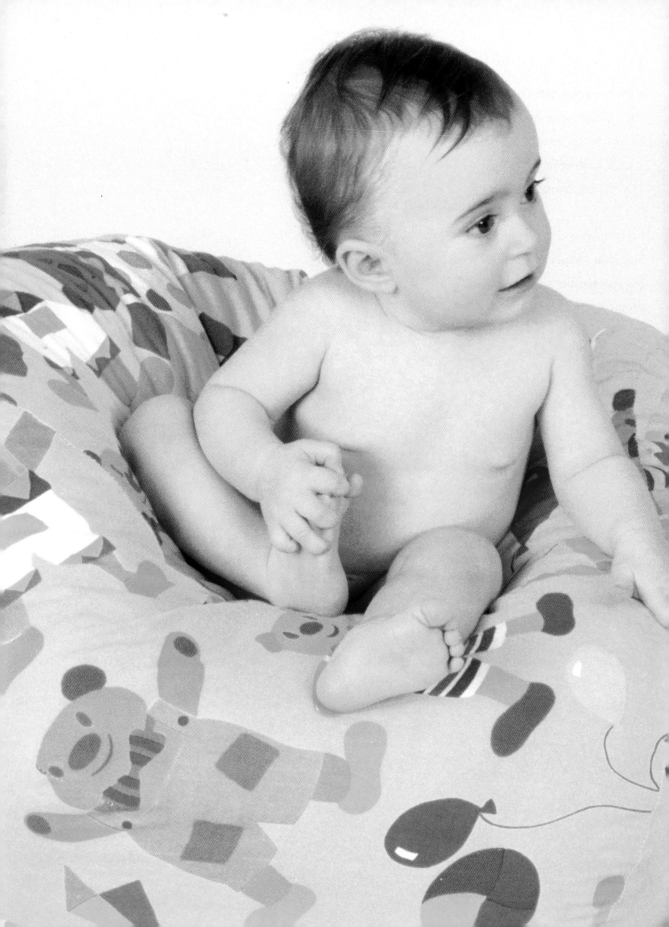

To develop the skills they need in life and to grow up happy and healthy, children need a safe and caring environment that stimulates them to learn. They need continued positive input from adults, starting from the early days.

In this book, Eileen Fursland offers ideas and activities which you can use to help your baby or child experience relaxation, touch, movement and exploration – all as part of everyday play. It will also help you – especially if you are a new parent – to understand how your baby or toddler's abilities will develop and how you can help him progress from one stage to the next.

If a child is to reach his full potential, a strong bond between parent and child is vital. Looking after a baby or toddler can be a challenge sometimes, even for the most devoted parent. Physical contact, cuddles, massages, rough and tumble play and having fun together help a happy, loving relationship to grow.

Eileen Fursland clearly enjoys playing with children and her enthusiasm shines through on every page. This is a book which doesn't talk down to you, or preach, or make you worry about whether you are doing the right thing. It simply aims to help you make the most of the time you spend playing with your child, by providing lots of inventive ideas for exploratory play from imaginative messy play to more active pursuits such as running, climbing and swimming.

In our technological environment, where many of the activities children enjoy involve sitting down, there is a danger that they may become inactive and ultimately unfit. But a child who learns to enjoy physical play from an early age is likely to carry on and have a more healthy, active adult life.

Children's Play is a positive and inspiring book with a whole host of play ideas which will appeal to parents and their babies and children everywhere.

Nikki Shack
Senior Paediatric Physiotherapist (Neurosciences)
Great Ormond Street Hospital for Children

About this Book

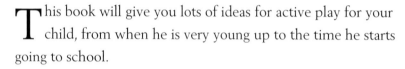

This book will give you lots of ideas for active play for your child, from when he is very young up to the time he starts going to school.

Your baby will sit, crawl, stand and walk when he is ready, and you can't make him do these things any earlier. What you can do is encourage him and come up with ways to help him practise his skills as they develop, by playing games together that you both enjoy. The aim is to have fun, not to help you produce a superbaby!

By encouraging active play in the pre-school years, you can get your child off to a good start and help him to grow up strong, supple, co-ordinated and confident. It also encourages him to enjoy physical activity - which is vital for his healthy development through childhood and for the rest of his life.

The exercises and games in this book don't involve setting aside a special time for a long routine. Looking after a child is busy enough without that! This isn't a textbook of complicated instructions that have to be followed rigidly. So just choose the ideas which appeal to you, or adapt them to suit you and your child, and I hope they will give you some inspiration whenever you have a few minutes to play together.

There are no rules apart from the obvious - don't move your

baby around too much just after a feed, and take your lead from him, watching for what he enjoys most and when he's had enough.

The book also gives you some insight into how babies' and toddlers' physical skills develop and an idea of what children can do at each stage. The ages given are only approximate - every child is an individual and develops at his or her own rate. There isn't a "right" time to learn to roll over, to sit, or to walk, for instance - there can be quite a big difference in the ages at which perfectly normal and healthy children develop the same skill. If you are concerned about your child, talk to your health visitor.

It's always nice when your baby learns to do something that he couldn't do before, but try to be patient. He will move on to the next new achievement when he is ready.

Each stage in your child's development brings its own joys and frustrations, may make you smile and fill you with pride or have you gritting your teeth and tearing your hair out. Most of all it will make you marvel at the amazing little person who has come to share your life.

Early Days

Your Baby's Life Before Birth

Moving moments

Before birth your baby floats in a kind of balloon of warm fluid inside your uterus. She begins to stretch her limbs as early as eight weeks. By the end of the third month of pregnancy she is fully formed, with fingers and toes, and all she has to do from then on is to get bigger and mature.

You won't be able to feel her at first, because she's so small that she can move around freely without touching the walls of your abdomen. Your own movements, however, may send her somersaulting around in the waters which surround her, inside your uterus.

As she grows bigger and the space gets a little more cramped, you'll start to feel her when she moves. The first movement you will be aware of may occur at around 18 or 20 weeks of pregnancy - but second-time mothers often recognize the sensations earlier. At first it is a little like a butterfly fluttering inside your abdomen, but later on it will feel like a definite kick.

At around 20 weeks she will start to settle into a pattern of activity and sleep - she may be at her most active when you are resting. By around 24 weeks the doctor or midwife should be able to tell, by feeling your abdomen, what position your baby is in. Towards the end of pregnancy, most babies settle into position with their head down. As your stomach gets bigger you'll be able to lie in the bath and watch lumps and bumps appearing as she changes position or tries to stretch her limbs.

By the end of pregnancy she is curled up in a ball, with her knees tucked up to her chin, her head forward on her chest and her arms crossed in front of her. She can no longer move her whole body, but you'll feel her trying to stretch her arms and legs. You may even feel her having the hiccups from time to time – it's like a ticking or rhythmic pulsation inside you.

What it's like for your baby

What is your baby experiencing inside the womb? At 26 to 28 weeks she opens her eyes for the first time, and can sense light and dark outside. If you were to go out in bright sunshine with a bare stomach she might be aware of a rosy glow. In winter when you are wearing thick clothes your baby is cocooned in darkness most of the time.

"I wasn't really aware of feeling my baby move until quite late on, about 23 weeks. I think I had probably felt him before, but I'd just put it down to wind!"
MELANIE

A foetus at five months

It's quite noisy for your baby inside the uterus. Sounds are muffled because of the amniotic fluid, but she can hear the pounding of your heart and digestive sounds as food moves around in your stomach and your intestines pump away. She'll be able to hear some sounds from outside too. Although she won't hear your voice clearly, she will get to know it by its tone and inflection - and if dad is around enough, she will get to know his voice too. From around 23 weeks she responds to sound - a loud noise nearby may make her jump. She may kick energetically when she hears music and can even learn to recognize certain music if she hears it frequently before she is born.

Researchers believe unborn babies can also respond to touch, so if you feel like doing it, sing to your baby or caress her by stroking your abdomen.

She practises crawling and even walking movements instinctively, opening and closing her eyes and using her lungs, though at this stage, of course, the latter are filled with fluid rather than air. By full term a baby is floating in around 10 pints of amniotic fluid. She drinks some of the fluid, and might even suck her thumb.

She's Here At Last!

New babies seem totally helpless but they are born with a set of reflexes, which means they can do certain things at birth. One important reflex is sucking, which a baby can do before birth. Although it takes some babies a couple of days to get going, many new babies have a strong urge to suck and will latch on to their mother's breast very soon after they are born.

The rooting reflex helps the baby find the breast. If something brushes against a newborn baby's cheek, she will

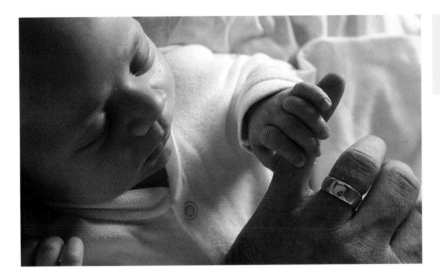

turn her head in that direction and open her mouth, searching for the nipple.

Like a baby animal, a newborn has a reflex that allows her to cling on to her mother. If you put your finger into your baby's palm, she will grasp it. She clings on so tightly with her fingers that you can even lift her upper body by the strength of her own grip. If you do this, make sure someone else has their hands behind her head, just in case she lets go.

At birth a baby also has stepping, crawling and walking reflexes. If you brush the front of the baby's shin against a hard surface such as the edge of a table, she will make a stepping movement as if to step up onto the surface. If you hold her in a standing position with her feet touching a surface she will make walking movements with her legs, putting one foot in front of the other, and when you put her on her tummy she will draw her legs up under her abdomen and may make movements which resemble crawling.

If your baby feels as though she is falling, she will react by flinging her arms and legs away from her body, with her fingers splayed out, then drawing them in again, with fists clenched. This is called the Moro reflex and is an instinctive action

The doctor will check your new baby's reflexes

triggered when new babies feel unsafe. At your newborn baby's first check-up, the doctor may test her Moro reflex, by holding her around the shoulders with one hand and supporting her head with the other, then allowing her head to fall by a few centimetres. Some of the other reflexes will also be tested, to make sure your baby's central nervous system is working as it should.

Some reflexes, such as sucking and rooting, have an obvious purpose while others, such as the walking and Moro reflex, don't. Almost all the newborn reflexes disappear as your baby matures. Rooting disappears in the first couple of weeks, the walking reflex disappears at five to six weeks, and the Moro reflex goes by around three to four months. Learned movements, which your baby wants to make, take the place of reflex movements over which she has no control.

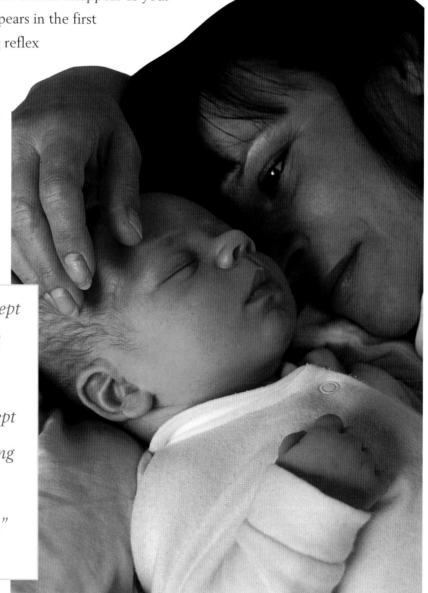

"On the first night I kept him in my bed and cuddled him. All through the night I kept waking up and looking at him - I couldn't believe he was mine."

SARAH

How To Handle Your Newborn Baby

New babies look so fragile that most new parents are a bit
nervous about handling them at first. But even if you feel all
fingers and thumbs in the first few days, it won't be long before
you are feeling more confident and actually enjoy handling her.

The main thing to remember is that you always need to
support your new baby's head. At this stage it's literally too
heavy for her back and neck muscles. When you are picking her
up or laying her down in her cot or holding or carrying her, keep
one hand behind her head to support it.

A baby has soft spots on the top of her head called the
fontanelles, where the bones of the skull have not yet fused. You
may even see a pulse beating inside the fontanelle at the front.
You can't hurt your baby by normal gentle handling of her
head, because the fontanelles are protected by a tough
membrane, but make sure young children don't poke them. And
no-one should ever shake a baby - it can damage the brain.

Handle her gently but firmly. Babies don't like sudden
movements. If you were to let her head fall back suddenly on
the mattress, for instance, she would respond with the Moro
reflex, splaying out her arms and legs.

Babies' joints are very flexible, so it's unlikely that you'll
hurt her by bending her limbs while you're dressing or
undressing her. You'll find dressing her easier if you lie her on a
firm surface, such as a changing table or on a blanket on the
floor. This leaves both your hands free. Talk or sing to her while
you're doing it, to reassure her.

If she cries when you are changing her or dressing her, it's
probably because she doesn't like the cool air on her skin. It
might help to lay a light cloth or blanket over her body when
she's uncovered. Putting a towel on the changing mat makes it a
warmer surface for her to lie on when you change her nappy.

Your baby will enjoy being carried and held against your body - it makes her feel warm and secure. Hold her against your chest, with her head on your shoulder. Alternatively, lie her back in your arms, resting her head in the crook of one of your arms and supporting her body with the other - her head should be slightly higher than her body.

Most parents instinctively tend to hold their babies on their left-hand side; this is thought to be because it's comforting for the baby to feel your heart beating, just like when she was in the womb.

Babies also enjoy gentle movement: being rocked, carried, pushed

Hold your baby facing you on your lap, sitting her up at a slight angle and cradling her head in your hands. This is the best way to get her attention. When you smile and talk to her she will look at your face - especially your eyes. Make your face expressive - if you put out your tongue or make a wide O-shape with your mouth, she may even try to imitate you.

in the pram or travelling in the car. Gently swaying to and fro, rocking or bobbing up and down while you are carrying her can help to settle her if she is crying. Try singing to her, and stroking or patting her back.

But if she is getting into a state, doing six things at once will make matters worse. Don't give her too much stimulation - be guided by how she responds.

Just because your baby can't talk doesn't mean she can't communicate with you. You will soon learn to read your baby's body language and be surprised by how much you understand her needs.

"Jake sucked his thumb on the day he was born, then he seemed to lose interest in his hands. Now, at nine weeks, he has started sucking his hand again."

MARIA

Cheyanne, 10 weeks old, likes to be held like this, especially when she is unsettled. Hold your baby under her arms, with her back against your body. Rock her to and fro to distract her - or try stroking her tummy with a circular movement in a clockwise direction. The gentle pressure will help to disperse any wind.

Sometimes she will be quiet and relaxed, lying fairly still, happy to watch the world go by; at other times she may tense up, perhaps because she's been unsettled by a loud noise. Crying is one signal you can't mistake. When she is hungry, lonely or has stomach ache she will cry. She will learn that this is a way of communicating her needs to you.

When your baby is wide awake and alert, and she's been fed, she is ready for outside stimulation - to look around, listen to sounds, and watch brightly-coloured mobiles or other things around her, especially you. If she is tired she may "switch off" and stare vacantly, usually a sign that she's had enough for the time being.

Babies differ in the way they respond to the world around them. Some babies are particularly sensitive to outside stimuli - noise, handling, lights. They feel bombarded. They can't shut out the stimuli as well as other babies can, and need a quieter, more protected environment. You will recognize your own baby's "style" by watching the way she behaves, and you'll get to know just what she needs.

This is another position that soothes some babies. Sitting down, lay your baby face down across your lap and gently rub her back in an up-and-down motion.

Stretching Out

Towards the end of pregnancy your baby had very little room to move in the womb. In the first few weeks after she is born, she will still adopt the classic foetal position, curled up with her arms and legs drawn into her body and her hands closed in fists most of the time. Although she may wriggle and wave her arms and legs about sometimes, she still feels most secure in this position and it will take a few weeks
before she uncurls.

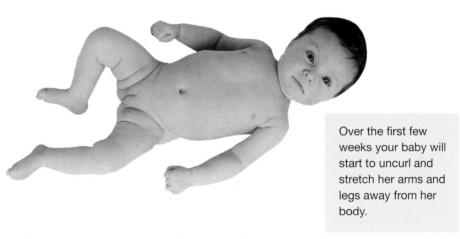

Over the first few weeks your baby will start to uncurl and stretch her arms and legs away from her body.

Premature babies are the exception. They are still quite small when they are born. Because they had plenty of space in the womb, they tend to stretch out more than babies born at full term.

At first babies don't have the muscular strength and co-ordination to do much more than turn their heads, but this gradually develops and they begin to have more control over their movements.

Your baby will start to wave her arms and legs about. At first, she tends to move her arms more than her legs. Her first kicks will be a bit jerky and random but as her muscle co-ordination develops she will make smoother and stronger

> *"He kept his legs curled up for a good three weeks. Then as he stretched out, he seemed to get longer all of a sudden."*
>
> LISA

bicycling movements. She will also start to open out her hands - by eight weeks they are open most of the time.

A newborn baby has a reflex that keeps her head turned to one side rather than in the middle when she is lying on her back. Your baby will be able to turn her head but for the first eight weeks or so you will find that she rarely keeps it in the middle.

In the first month your baby may be able to raise her head for a few seconds when she is lying on her front. At six to eight weeks, if you hold her sitting slightly propped up on your lap, she'll be able to hold her head up for a few seconds by herself.

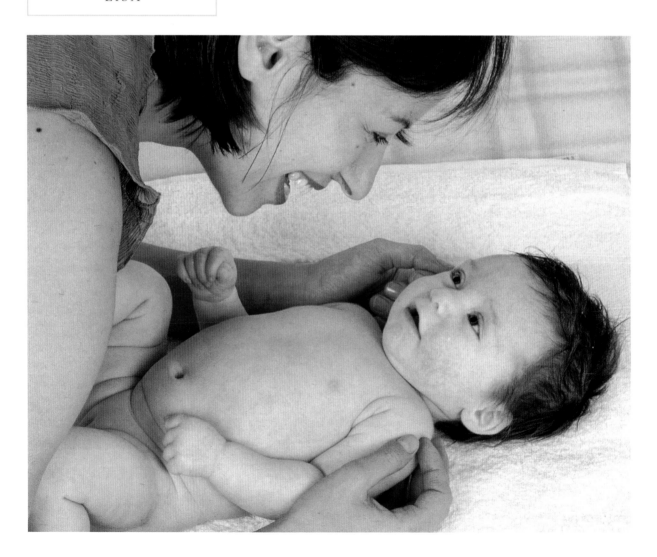

Hearing And Eyesight

Although she can hear sounds even before birth, it isn't until four or five weeks of age that your baby starts looking towards the source of the sounds she hears.

A baby can't see clearly at first, because the retina at the back of the eye, the optic nerve (which carries the signals to the brain) and the relevant part of the brain are not fully developed. In fact, an adult with the vision of a newborn baby would be classed as blind.

Your baby can see what's important to her and it's no accident that she can focus best on things that are about 20 to 25 centimetres (8-10 inches) away - the distance to your face when she is breastfeeding. Her ability to focus gradually improves.

If a slow-moving object enters your baby's field of vision, her eyes will lock onto it and follow it until it disappears from view. This is called "tracking". Early on, this process will be slow and jerky, her eyes often lagging behind whatever she is looking at and then catching up, and she cannot see out of the corners of her eyes. In the first few weeks this ability improves and her tracking becomes more accurate.

She is very sensitive to light at first so in the first few weeks she will dislike being near bright or flashing lights.

If she's lying in her cot or on the floor, give her a mobile, a toy or something else that's interesting to look at, within her focussing range. Early on she can see black and white, strong contrasts and strong, primary colours best. Pastels won't make any impression on her.

In the first three months she also starts to understand cause and effect - that she can make things happen with her own actions. This might be kicking her legs against some tissue paper to produce a rustling sound, shaking a rattle to make a noise, or simply smiling and cooing at you to make you smile back.

Facing your baby, slowly move your head by leaning from one side to the other. Your baby will follow you with her eyes or, as she gains more control over her head movements, she will turn her head to watch you.

Alternatively hold up a toy and move that. Your baby will just as readily "track" that across her field of vision.

Learning To Love You

"Bonding" - the process by which parents and their offspring learn to love each other - is just as important for a baby's long-term well-being as food and warmth.

It doesn't have to start at birth, though it often does. Some mothers are overwhelmed with love for their babies at first sight, while for others these feelings take longer to grow.

If the birth went well and your baby was born alert, she may respond to you straight away by looking at you and perhaps having her first breast-feed soon after birth. You can hold her and cuddle her, explore her tiny fingers and toes and marvel at the little miracle you have produced. But sometimes mothers are too exhausted to feel anything but relief that it's all over, and babies are too sleepy or, if there are problems, may have to stay in a special care baby unit.

Even if the start of that special relationship has to be delayed for a little while, over the next few weeks and months it will develop as you care for your baby, feed her, talk to her, tune in to her needs, her likes and dislikes and show her that she can trust you and depend on you.

Your baby will learn to associate the sight of you with your voice, your smell - a breastfed baby can recognize the smell of her mother's milk just a few days after birth - and the comforting feeling of being in your arms and being fed. She'll soon realize that you're the one who does all those nice things for her. You are completely besotted with her - and it won't be long before she returns the compliment.

Babies are "programmed" to be interested in people right from birth. Your baby will spend a lot of time watching you over the first few weeks. A baby would rather look at a face than anything else. She even prefers to look at a pattern in the shape of a face rather than a random pattern. She is a sociable

"In the first week her eyes were quite fluttery and all over the place. She would look at my face but couldn't hold her gaze for long. After the first week she started to focus on my face a lot more."

PRAVINI

Your baby will enjoy the close contact of a sling. Some mothers find that, snuggled up to them for long periods, their babies are more content and cry less.

little thing. A baby also has an in-built preference for voices over other sounds. Adults trying to get a baby's attention automatically use a higher pitch when they are speaking, and babies are more responsive to this - probably because they are conditioned in the womb to their mother's voice, and female voices are higher than men's.

One day, between around four and six weeks, you will be rewarded for all your hard work with her first smile. At first she smiles at everyone equally. But by around three months of age it will be clear that she knows you're her mum and she responds to you differently from people who are unfamiliar.

Physical contact is essential for a new baby - she wants to be near you and when you hold, cuddle and carry her, she feels safe and secure. Some babies like to be carried round most of the time, and cry when they are put down. Many babies have a "fussy" period between around three and 12 weeks when they seem to cry a lot for no apparent reason, often at the end of the day. Sometimes carrying them round is the only thing that will soothe them.

Some mothers find that carrying their baby in a sling works well. "Wearing" your baby like this, rather than leaving her in a baby chair or cot, means your baby has the close contact with you that she wants, and you have both hands free to get on with things. In some cultures, of course, babies are carried round constantly on their mothers' backs while the mothers work in the fields.

Your baby will study your face intently. Make your face and voice as expressive as you can when you talk to her. A baby quickly learns about "taking turns" when she interacts with you - she will respond to what you have said by waving her arms and legs or cooing and smiling. Then she will pause for a moment so you can have your "turn" to say something else. It's just the start of many conversations.

Playing

At first it seems as though it's all feeding and sleeping but after the third or fourth week, you will have more time between your baby's feeds and sleeps to play with her. She will start to spend more time awake and wanting to be entertained.

You will need to vary the positions you put your baby in to enable her to watch what's going on around her. Changing her sitting or lying position will stop her getting bored and uncomfortable, and also give her the chance to exercise different groups of muscles.

Sometimes she will be happiest lying on her back in the cot or on the floor. Babies should be placed on their backs, not their fronts, to sleep - this has been found to reduce the risk of cot death. On her back she will find a cosy, curled up position she likes. That doesn't mean you can't put your baby on her front to play, while she's awake. In fact, it is a good idea to put her on her front sometimes, because it gives her the opportunity to exercise different muscles and strengthens her back.

Between nappy changes she might enjoy being allowed to lie on her back and kick without a nappy (put an old towel or a nappy underneath her in case of accidents).

From around six weeks she can sit propped up in her bouncing chair for a good view of the room. But sitting like this is more tiring for her than lying flat, so alternate the seat with periods on the floor. Up to the age of six weeks she shouldn't sit in a bouncing baby chair for longer than around ten minutes at a time, because it's better for her spine if she lies flat for most of the time that you're not holding her. If you don't have a pram, you need a pushchair that fully reclines until your baby is at least three months old.

For travelling in the car, first-stage, rear-facing infant carriers are suitable for babies from birth to around nine

In the first few weeks your baby's main activity will be looking - mobiles and bright, shiny things that move will attract her attention best.

months. These seats are designed to support a newborn baby's spine. If your baby is so small that she can't sit squarely in the seat and she flops forwards or to one side, give her extra support with a head-support cushion (this may come with the seat or you can buy them separately) or with rolled-up towels tucked down each side.

Babies shouldn't sleep on their front, but they do need to spend some time on their front while they are awake. Put her in this position for a few minutes at a time, as a change from lying on her back. She will use different muscles when she's lying on her front.

Remember, too, that your baby can't move around to make herself more comfortable when she's in a car seat. When you take her on a long car journey, stop every so often and take her out so she can lie flat on the back seat and kick her legs for a while.

There are some places you shouldn't put your baby: don't leave her baby seat on a high surface such as the kitchen table, because as she moves or bounces it could fall off. Never put your baby on the bed or on a sofa and leave her there alone, because she can fall off even before she has learned to roll over.

While she is lying in her cot or on the floor give her brightly coloured things to look at within her

She won't be able to grasp a rattle and shake it until later on, but a wrist rattle which fastens around her wrist makes a noise when she moves, which will attract her attention.

One day she will discover her hands and realize they are part of her - she will lie there, completely absorbed, studying her hands and opening and closing them.

focussing range, otherwise she will just gaze into the distance. A baby gym is ideal, and at around four months she will start to reach out and try to bat the toys on it. She will enjoy looking into a baby mirror, too, though, of course, she won't realize who she's looking at.

She will soon start to enjoy her bath - being in water is an interesting, new sensation and will give her a chance to kick her legs around without being encumbered by nappy and clothes. When you feel confident, it's lovely to have your baby in the big bath with you as well - but make sure the temperature of the water suits her, not you.

When you are bathing or changing her, introduce her to her fingers and toes. You'll find that some of the old rhymes from your childhood, like "This little piggy went to market", will start coming back to you.

You are your baby's best plaything - your cuddles and rocking, your face, your voice, your smiles, are what she likes best of all.

> ⚠ **Take Care**
> **Never pass a hot drink to anyone over your baby's head.**

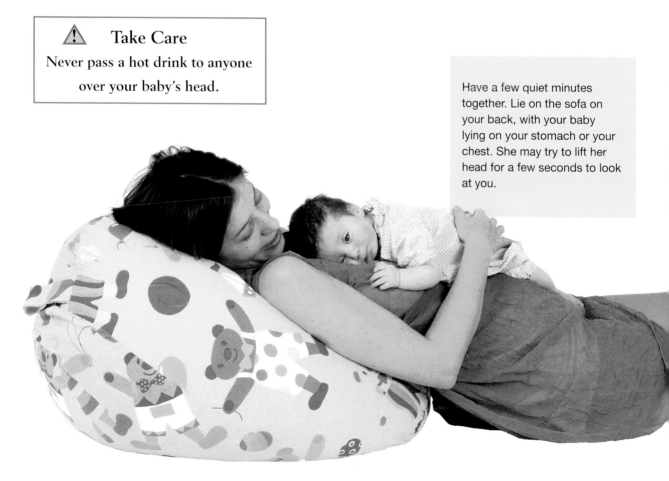

Have a few quiet minutes together. Lie on the sofa on your back, with your baby lying on your stomach or your chest. She may try to lift her head for a few seconds to look at you.

Massaging Your Baby

"When I first started gently stroking Harry after his bath, he hated it. He didn't like to have his clothes off until he was about a month old. Now he loves to lie there with nothing on, and he is getting used to the idea of massage."

DIANE

Massage can be a special time that you and your baby both enjoy.
You can start to massage your baby when he is just two or three weeks old. It's a good way of getting to know him and becoming more confident at handling him.

Your baby will enjoy the physical contact and closeness of a massage. It will help relax him, keep his joints flexible and encourage muscle co-ordination. It's also good for his digestion and circulation. Some experts believe it can promote his motor development by stretching out his limbs and encouraging movement. Choose a time between feeds when your baby is not sleepy, and do it in a warm room, with warm hands. Take off any jewellery that could scratch him.

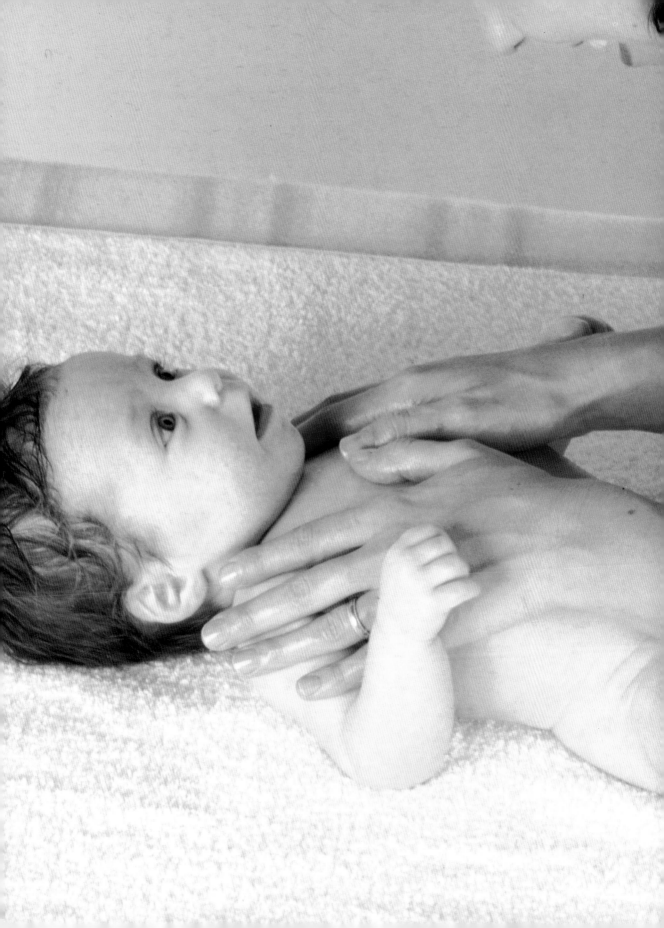

In the first few weeks many babies don't like to be undressed. But even a young baby can enjoy a light massage when she doesn't mind lying with no clothes on for a few minutes. Try gently stroking her chest and arms, or her back and legs. When she is happy to be undressed for longer, you can do the full massage routine that begins opposite.

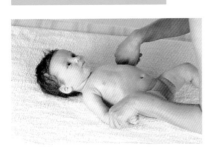

You need to use an oil that is absorbed into the skin - not baby oil, but something like olive oil (from the supermarket) or almond oil. Before you start, check that your baby isn't allergic to the oil by putting it on a small patch of skin and leaving it for 30 minutes.

Get into a comfortable position, for instance sitting on a cushion with your legs splayed and your baby in the middle; leaning back against a cushion or chair and massaging your baby on your raised knees; or kneeling on a cushion or on the floor, with your bottom between your feet. To avoid backache, sit so that you can keep your back straight while you lean forward to do the massage.

Put a nappy or old towel underneath your baby in case of accidents, and lay him on a towel. Put some oil on your hands and rub them together. Do this throughout the massage whenever you need to, so your hands glide easily over his skin.

When he is very young, use your fingers, flat against his body. As soon as he's big enough, use your whole hand. Try to keep as much of your hands in contact with your baby's body as you can when you are massaging him.

To start with, you can just massage one part of his body and build up to the whole-body routine opposite when you are more confident. Be guided by your baby's responses - adapt your rhythm and pressure when you see what he seems to like. Start with a gentle and slow touch with a young baby. Older babies tend to prefer firmer and faster rhythms. Only carry on for as long as your baby is enjoying it.

Most of your massage strokes will be outwards from the body - the opposite from adult massage. This is because babies tend to be curled in and need to be encouraged to stretch out. Talk and sing to your baby as you massage him.

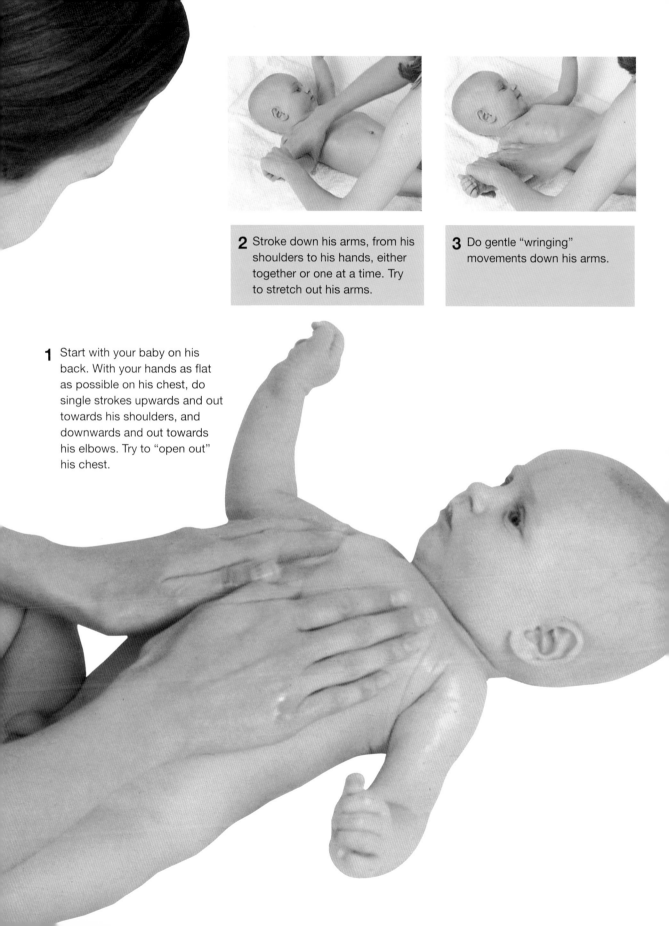

2 Stroke down his arms, from his shoulders to his hands, either together or one at a time. Try to stretch out his arms.

3 Do gentle "wringing" movements down his arms.

1 Start with your baby on his back. With your hands as flat as possible on his chest, do single strokes upwards and out towards his shoulders, and downwards and out towards his elbows. Try to "open out" his chest.

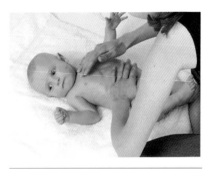

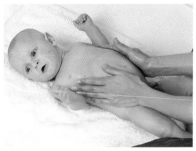

4 Do single downward strokes from his chest to his tummy.

5 Do circular movements clockwise around his tummy, using one or both hands.

6 Massage with downward strokes from the sides of his body towards his tummy.

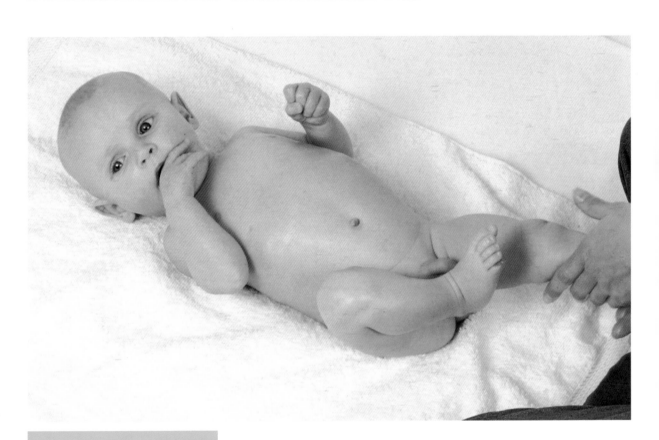

7 Stroke down his legs, one at a time or both together. Gently straighten them out.

Do "wringing" movements down his legs.

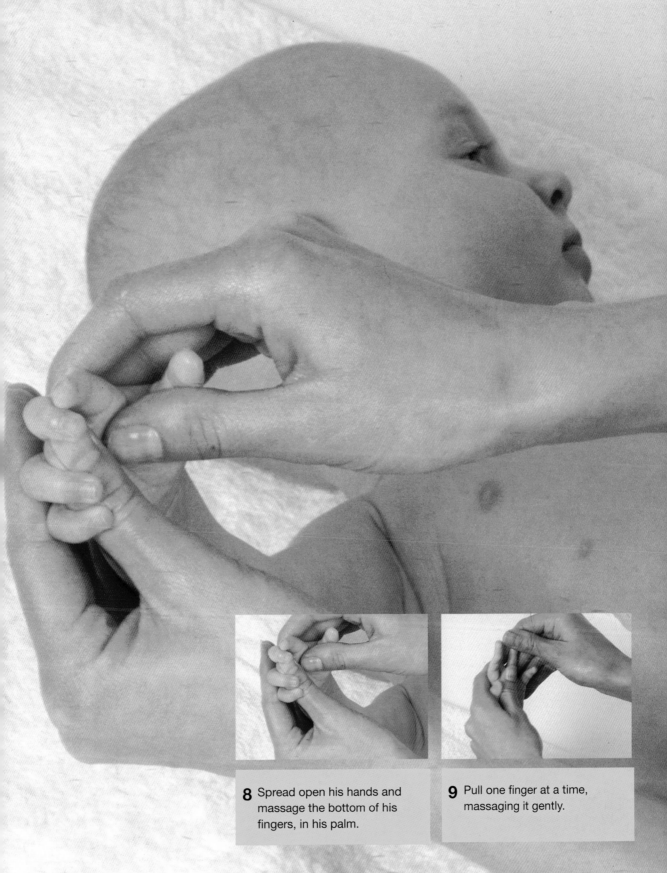

8 Spread open his hands and massage the bottom of his fingers, in his palm.

9 Pull one finger at a time, massaging it gently.

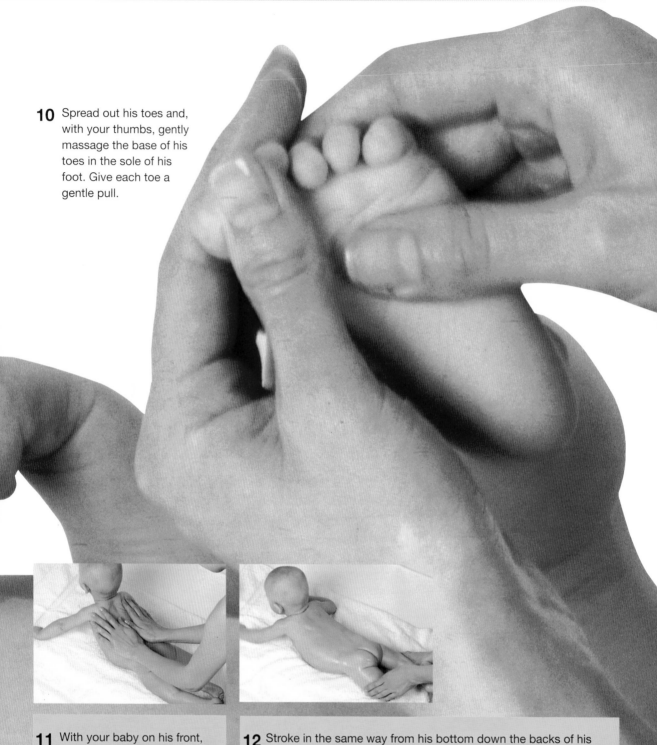

10 Spread out his toes and, with your thumbs, gently massage the base of his toes in the sole of his foot. Give each toe a gentle pull.

11 With your baby on his front, keeping your hands flat, do single strokes down from his shoulders to his bottom.

12 Stroke in the same way from his bottom down the backs of his legs and then gently massage his bottom with the heel of your hands, in a circular movement.
- Continue stroking down the backs of his legs to his feet.

Your baby might also like to have his face massaged (don't use the oil for this in case it gets into his eyes). Rhythmically stroke upwards from his chin, round his cheeks and to the centre of his forehead. Using your thumbs, massage around his eyes, along his eyebrows to his temples. Then gently massage his head as if you were shampooing his hair.

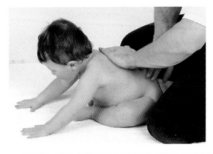 

An older baby like Jedd, above, might not want to lie still. But you can still give him a massage if he prefers to sit up - most of the moves here can be adapted for a more active baby.

Looking Around and Taking Notice

Lifting His Head

One of the earliest movements a newborn baby can make is to arch his head and turn it from side to side if a soft cloth is placed over his face. This is an important protective reflex, to keep his mouth and nose clear so he can breathe. Conscious movements

that are under his control develop in the first few weeks.

Your baby can't hold up his floppy head at all at first. But at just a few weeks old, he will start to raise his head for a few seconds when he is lying on his front. Gradually, as his muscles get stronger, he will be able to lift it higher and for longer periods. As he develops more control over his head, when he is lying on his back he starts to keep it in the middle rather than always turning it to the side as he used to do in the first two to three months.

All babies gain control over their movements in the same sequence, starting with the head and moving downwards. The ability to lift the head is followed by lifting the shoulders and gaining control over the arms and hands. Between six and eight months he develops muscular control far enough down his spine to be able to sit unsupported. Last of all his legs become strong enough for him to crawl and eventually to walk. This process of gaining control over movement always happens in the same order, though of course some babies go through it more quickly than others. So, believe it or not, lifting his head is the first stage in learning to walk!

By six to eight weeks he can lie on his back, waving his arms around and bicycling with his legs. This strengthens his muscles, getting them ready for crawling and walking later. When you pull him up into a sitting position by his arms, his head lags behind only briefly as those neck and back muscles continue to grow stronger.

Lie opposite your baby on the floor, so you are facing each other, and talk to her. At two months old she will raise her head slightly to look at you.

Try this exercise when your
baby can hold his head up by
himself.
• Lay him on the floor and let him
grasp your thumbs while you
hold him around the wrist and
forearms, and gently raise him
into a sitting position.

He'll enjoy the feeling of being
pulled up. At five or six months
old he will be able to keep his
head upright and his back
straight.

There isn't much parents can do to speed things up -
your baby will develop at his own rate and won't start to
hold his head up until he is ready. The best way to help is
by giving him the opportunity to move freely, by playing
with him and by supplying lots of interesting things for
him to look or aim at, and reach for. Whatever he's trying
to do, your encouragement and praise will spur him on to
greater achievements.

Ivan is five months old and his
arms are just about strong
enough to support his upper
body, but not for long.

Using His Hands

Your baby's growing hand skills will open up a new world of interesting things for him to explore. If your baby tends to keep his hands closed in a fist for a lot of the time, you can encourage him to open them up and uncurl his fingers by gently stroking the backs of his hands. Try rubbing his palm against something with an interesting texture, such as fur. The sooner he opens up his hands, the sooner he can start playing with them.

He will lie in his cot watching his hands and fingers as he moves them - this is the first step towards learning hand-eye co-ordination, which he will need when he starts reaching for toys. But his hands are his most easily accessible toy and he will make the most of them, exploring one hand with the other and putting his fingers or fists in his mouth to suck. Even before he can actually reach for something, you may find that if you touch his hand with something he's interested in, his arm will jerk towards it.

From around three months old your baby will be able to hold something for a short time if you put it in his hand. Rattles are useful at this stage, because they draw his attention to the fact that there is something in his hand. Eventually he will make the connection between waving his hand and the noise that it makes.

Using his hands in front of his body is called "midline play" and starts at three to four months. You can encourage this by sitting him semi-upright and giving him a toy or rattle that he will hold in both hands.

At around four months he will probably start trying to take hold of things himself. If you dangle a toy in front of him, he will throw out his hands towards it and if it touches his hand, he will close his hand around it.

A few weeks later, he will deliberately reach for a toy,

grasp it and, if he can, he'll pull it towards him and put it in his mouth. He has realized that if he can see something he can touch it, handle it, move it about and taste it. He is learning how to investigate things. Watch out - he will want to investigate you, and will grab at your nose, chin, earrings and glasses, and pull handfuls of your hair.

Up to the age of around six months, he uses his whole hand in a mitten-like action to get hold of a toy, raking the object into his palm. It's not until later on that he can use his fingers and thumbs in a pincer movement, or adjust his hand to the shape of the toy.

His aim, when he reaches for a toy, is not very accurate at first. At about four months he can focus on objects several feet away and as his 3-D vision improves, he gets better at hitting his target. With both eyes working together, he can judge depth and distances better. His two-handed reach will progress into a more accurate one-handed reach, and by around six months he won't need to look at his own hand any more when he's reaching for something.

Sitting your baby in a semi-upright position makes it easier for him to use his hands. Lying flat, he tends to look to the side, cycling with his legs and waving his arms about and if he wants to use his hands he has to lift his arms against gravity. If he is sitting semi-upright in your arms or in a baby seat, his head faces forwards. This posture encourages his hands and arms to come together in front of his body, so that he can play with his hands or with a toy. Choose lightweight toys that are easy to grip, so he can hold them for longer without dropping them.

How To Help

The best way you can help your baby to develop his manipulative skills is simply by providing him with a variety of safe, interesting things that he will be eager to grab and hold.

For a young baby, try suspending some bright toys or objects on a safe string across his cot within arm's reach, so he can practise swiping and making them move. If they make a noise when they move, even better. But never leave him alone with dangling things like this, just in case he gets his finger caught in the string or pulls it down.

A baby gym gives him lots of bright and interesting things to swipe at or kick.

There will come a time when he'll get frustrated with things that move away when he touches them. Then he will enjoy playing with activity centres or cradle gyms that fix to his cot, squeezy, squeaky toys and "feely" toys with lots of different textures for him to explore. You can give him different pieces of fabric, such as velvet and satin, to feel.

Playing with bricks is a wonderful game and a learning exercise for your baby from around five months. Bricks are small enough for him to pick up with one hand and perfect for him to practise grabbing. From six or seven months, he will start to bang with them and transfer them from one hand to the other.

Encourage his awareness of his hands with games and songs like "Pat-a-cake" and "Round and round the garden". Show him how to clap his hands!

Dangle an interesting toy in front of your baby's face within reaching distance and watch him go for it with both hands, gathering it in towards his body. Keep it still - at this stage he can't grab a moving toy.

Hold a toy out for your baby to take. He may look between his hand and the toy, trying to decide how to bring the two together. Be patient - give him time to judge the distance between his hand and the object. Don't make it too easy for him - let him reach for it before you hand it to him.

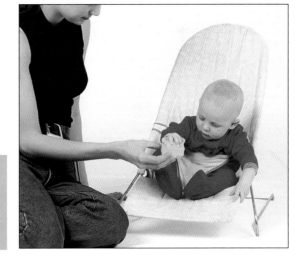

⚠ Watch Out

- When your baby starts making lightning grabs at everything within reach, keep dangerous things well out of his way - and never hold a hot drink and your baby at the same time.
- Babies put everything in their mouths, so never give your baby anything small enough to put in his mouth - he could choke on it. Don't leave him alone to play with things like ribbon or wool, because it could get wound round his neck, or around his fingers or toes, and cut off the blood supply.

To explore a toy, he uses his mouth as well as his hands.

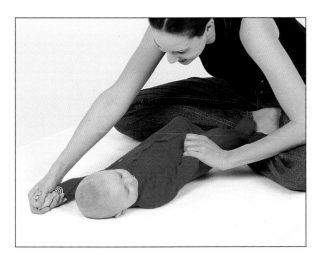

Lay your baby on his back and let him hold your thumbs. Raise his arms one at a time above his head and back down to his sides again.

Let's Work Out!

By the age of three months or so, your baby is much less wobbly than when he was born. Over the next three months his movements become stronger and smoother and he becomes quite active. He can sit in a supported position for longer and hold his head up. And he starts to make some of the movements that will eventually lead to crawling.

Even though he can move more for himself now, you need to vary the positions you put him in while he is playing or watching you around the house, so that he doesn't get bored or tired. He is spending more time awake and there are other ways he can play - both with you and by himself.

With your baby on his back, cross his arms over his body and stretch them out again to the sides.

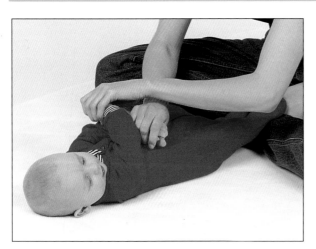

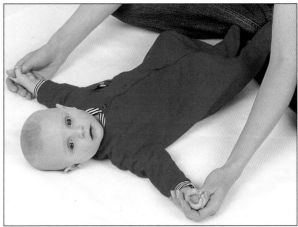

He will enjoy sitting in a baby seat, on your lap or propped up on the sofa (don't leave him there alone though, in case he falls off). He still needs a baby chair that is tilted back at this stage - until a baby can sit by himself, anything too upright will make him slump forward.

He can also play on the floor, on his front or back. Even though he can't yet crawl, he will surprise you by how far he can travel, either by shuffling or rolling.

There's quite a wide variation in the age at which babies roll over - some are content to stay where they are and don't make any attempt to roll, others are more active and squirmy and end up rolling over without even trying.

Stand him up on your lap or on the floor, holding him under his arms. He'll enjoy the feeling of standing up on his own two feet. At first his legs will soon buckle. Older babies will be able to stand supported for a few seconds, holding your hands, and will try to bounce - though of course they can't balance yet.

Clap his feet together, then raise them up towards his chest.

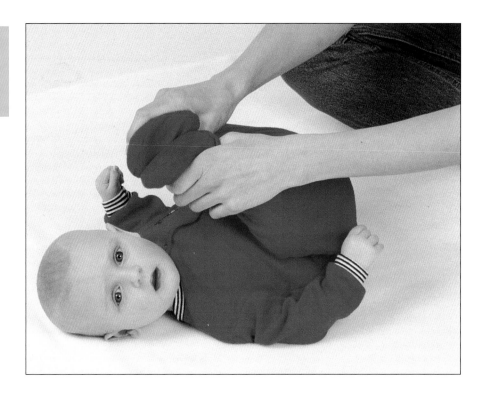

Often a baby goes through quite a frustrating period before he learns to crawl and before he can sit up on his own. He can see all sorts of fascinating things but can't get to them - and he wants to sit up but he can't balance by himself. He may want to be on your lap all the time. You may well find yourself longing for the time when he can sit and play by himself.

He will love it when you pull him up to a sitting or standing position. Towards the age of six months or so, if he isn't sitting alone, you can help him sit up but his back will still be rounded and he'll need his hands on the floor to stop himself falling over, so he won't be happy like this for long.

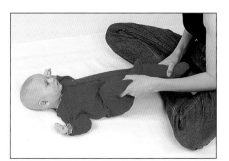

"Bicycle" with his legs in both directions, and then let him push against your hands with his feet.

Lots of babies enjoy physical play. It satisfies a baby's need to move around at a time when he can't do it by himself. He'll love to be tickled, swung around, "flown" through the air and bounced on your knee or on your lower legs. Or carry him while you dance around the room to music. When you're playing with your baby now, you don't have to be as gentle as when he was very young. But all babies are individuals and have their own likes and dislikes - be guided by your baby's response as to how boisterous you should be.

"When I put Anna down on the floor she doesn't stay in one place any more - even though she can't crawl yet, she can get right across the room by rolling."

ALICE

Show your baby how to roll over. Put a toy to one side of him to encourage him to look in that direction, then gently guide his hip over until he rolls on to his front.

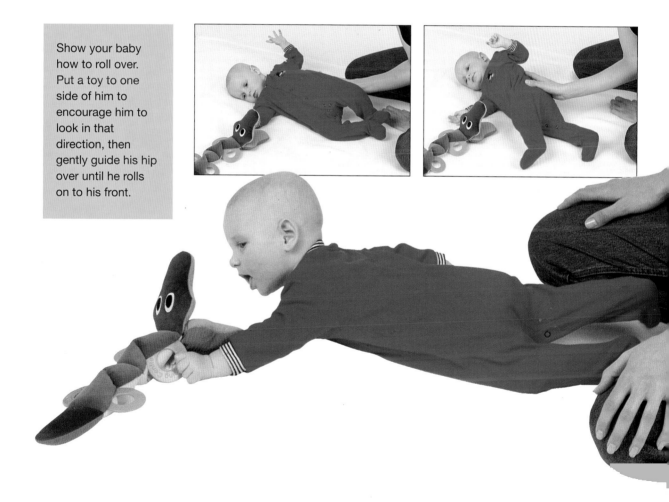

Lie flat on the floor and hold your baby around his chest. Bring him close to your face and then stretch out your arms to make him "go away again". (Add your own sound effects for extra excitement!)

The movement games and gentle exercises shown here - and other kinds of physical play - increase your baby's awareness of what he can do with his body. They will help develop his strength and co-ordination, keep his joints wonderfully flexible, help him learn to balance, and improve his confidence. But more important than all these, physical play is fun.

Choose a time when your baby is ready to play, not too hungry, and not just after a meal. Don't carry on with any exercise your baby doesn't enjoy.

Lie your baby over a large beach ball, and gently roll it to and fro. This will help develop his sense of balance.

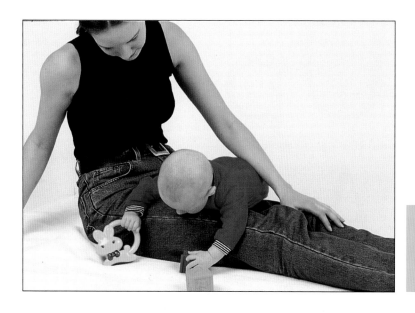

A baby who can't sit up yet might enjoy playing in this position. Use your legs to support his chest so his hands are free to play with a toy.

Baby Bouncers

Many babies love to bob around in a baby bouncer. Most baby bouncers need to be clamped to the doorframe, but some fit onto a freestanding frame. The baby is suspended in a harness so he can jump up and down.

Baby bouncers are generally suitable for babies from around four to five months who have good head control. Look at the manufacturers' guidelines but also assess your own baby's development. If you're not sure, have a word with your health visitor.

Make sure that your baby can put his feet flat on the floor so that he can take his weight properly as he bounces. And don't leave him in it for more than half an hour at a time.

 Beware - Baby On The Floor

At the stage when your baby can roll or shuffle around on the floor, you need to take some precautions:

- Keep the carpets clear of small bits he might put in his mouth.
- Protect him from a bumped head by guarding any sharp corners of fireplaces and so on with cushions.
- Watch out for anything dangerous he could grab and pull onto himself, such as a flimsy coffee table or the flex of a lamp.
- Use safety plugs in sockets.

Up, Up and Away

During the second half of her first year, a baby gets more and more of her body off the ground - first her top half, as she learns to sit by herself, and later on the rest of her body as she learns to stand and eventually to walk. From now on your baby will spend less time sitting on your lap or being carried and more time playing on the floor and exploring the house.

How Your Baby Learns To Sit

To sit unsupported your baby needs two things: enough strength in her back muscles to be able to keep her back straight, and the ability to balance so she doesn't topple over.

The first stage in learning to sit is leaning forwards, using both arms in front for support. Next, the baby straightens her back and manages not to topple backwards or forwards, and by around six or seven months she can sit for short periods without supporting herself with her hands.

But at first when she tries to play in this position, she will fall over. As she gets better at it, she might be able to play with a toy that is right in front of her, but if she twists round or

reaches too far for a toy, she is still likely to topple over
sideways or backwards. From around eight months she will
learn to put her hands out to the sides to save herself. It takes
quite a bit of practice before a baby can sit confidently and do
other things at the same time. Until she is about nine months
old, she will still need help in getting into a sitting position from
lying down.

Before he can sit
confidently by himself,
he will enjoy being in an
upright position to play.

You can help by putting her into a sitting position so she can practise, and propping her up with cushions when she's still learning to sit. This gives her support around her bottom and ensures that she doesn't hurt herself when she does collapse. As her balance improves, let her sit with cushions surrounding her, rather than supporting her, just in case of falls. Falling onto a hard surface will make her lose confidence. (Never leave your baby alone in a pile of cushions in case she falls into it face first.)

Babies find it easier to amuse themselves once they can sit up on their own and play with toys using both hands.

Games where your baby sits on your lap as you gently rock, bounce or sway your legs will help develop his sense of balance. At the same time, sing him a nursery rhyme like "To market, to market, to buy a fat pig" or "Ride a cock-horse to Banbury Cross".

Try playing "Row, row, row the boat" on the floor with your baby, holding him by his hands as you rock backwards and forwards together

When he is learning to sit, you can use your legs to support him - he could sit between them, leaning back against you, or let him lean forwards over your leg while he plays with toys in front of him.

Pushalong toys

A baby who is just starting to walk will enjoy a pushalong toy. These come in all shapes, sizes and colours from traditional wooden trolleys and toy dogs on wheels to brightly coloured pushalongs that start off as an activity centre for your baby to play with on the floor and convert to a wheeled toy when she starts to walk.

Being able to stand on her own two feet while steadying herself with the help of a pushalong toy gives a baby confidence and encourages her to start moving around the room. It lets her practise, safely, the skills she needs to walk alone.

At first you'll need to keep a careful eye on her in case the pushalong runs away from her too fast, but as she gets better at walking she will enjoy her new-found mobility and the feeling of importance as she trundles the toy around the room.

Make sure she doesn't fall and hurt herself by trying to push it down steps. And be prepared for some wear and tear on your furniture and skirting boards as she rams her pushalong toy into them!

Toddlers love to put things into a trolley or compartment and push them around the room or the garden, and these toys have quite a long life - children still enjoy playing with them long after they can walk perfectly well by themselves.

Note: Babywalkers - a seat on wheels which enables younger babies to propel themselves around the room before they are ready to walk are not recommended by the Child Accident Prevention Trust and the Royal Society for the Prevention of Accidents.

This is how many babies start to crawl. Sitting on the floor, Georgina notices a toy to one side of her. Lunging sideways to reach it and folding her legs into her body, she goes a bit too far and either falls on her tummy or finds herself on all fours. During the stage when your baby is practising lunging like this, give her soft toys to reach for - falling on top of a hard toy is no fun.

On The Move

At this stage your baby is on the move. She may start to make movements that will eventually progress to crawling - shuffling along on her tummy, pivoting round in a circle on her tummy, manoeuvring herself forwards by digging her fingers and toes into the carpet and squirming along, or getting on all fours and rocking backwards and forwards. Some babies shuffle backwards on their tummies at first, because their arms are stronger and better co-ordinated than their legs.

She may also get into a crawling position, drawing her knees up under her and leaning on her outstretched arms, and start "revving". The trouble is, it can be quite a few weeks before she actually goes anywhere. It's only when she develops sufficient strength in her hips and shoulders that she will really start to crawl.

Most babies start to crawl some time in the second six months. But not all babies do - some start walking without ever having crawled.

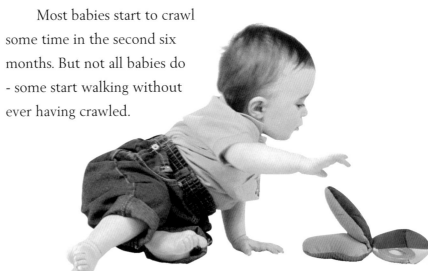

Many babies develop their own distinctive style - rather than crawling on all fours, they will shuffle around on one knee, pushing themselves along with the other foot, or crawl on hands and feet instead of hands and knees. Your baby might adopt

Give her a moving toy
or a ball to crawl after.

different styles depending on the surface she's crawling on.
Some babies find they can get along better shuffling on
their tummies with their elbows bent and their legs
straight, or by sliding on their bottoms on a polished floor.

The most efficient and fastest crawling style is when the arm on
one side and the leg on the opposite side move forwards together. The
baby uses one side of her body to balance the other.   But if this isn't
your baby's style, it's not something you can teach her.

Until she can crawl well, she may tend to collapse onto her tummy and cry until you come and put her back in a sitting position. Later, she learns to do it herself.

A crawling baby can reach all sorts of fascinating things she couldn't get at before - your sewing box, the cat's dinner, a precious ornament. If you haven't already done so, this really is the time to childproof your home. Move beyond her reach anything that is valuable, breakable, sharp or otherwise potentially harmful. Fit safety catches on cupboards, a fireguard and safety gates at the top and bottom of the stairs.

Don't leave her on her own - you need to keep an eye on her all the time. A playpen is the only safe place to leave her if, for instance, you have to answer the door, but she won't want to be confined to a playpen for long once she has learned to crawl.

When she is ready to crawl there are some things you can do to help. Put your baby in trousers rather than a dress or short pants - crawling, even on carpet, can be quite hard on bare knees. As far as you can, give her freedom to crawl around and explore the house. Making the rooms as safe as possible reduces the number of

Georgina, eight and a half months, enjoys negotiating a beanbag...

times you have to say "No" to her or move her away from something she mustn't have, and makes life less frustrating for you both.

She might enjoy crawling through a tunnel or an opened-up cardboard box, or over piles of cushions. Get down on all fours and join in with her, or play hide-and-seek around the furniture. And, finally, lots of encouragement will spur her on - whenever she learns to do something new, praise her and share her pleasure in her new achievement.

...and an even trickier obstacle!

Join in and have a crawling race with your baby, or chase her round the room.

Fear Of Falling?

American psychologist Joseph Campos found that babies develop a fear of heights when they start crawling. For his experiment he constructed a "visual cliff" with two chequered surfaces, one much lower than the other, and a sheet of transparent material over the top. It looks to the baby as though there is a sheer drop, although in reality there is no drop at all. Babies who had not yet learned to crawl were not afraid of dangling over the "edge", but those who could crawl held back, afraid of falling.

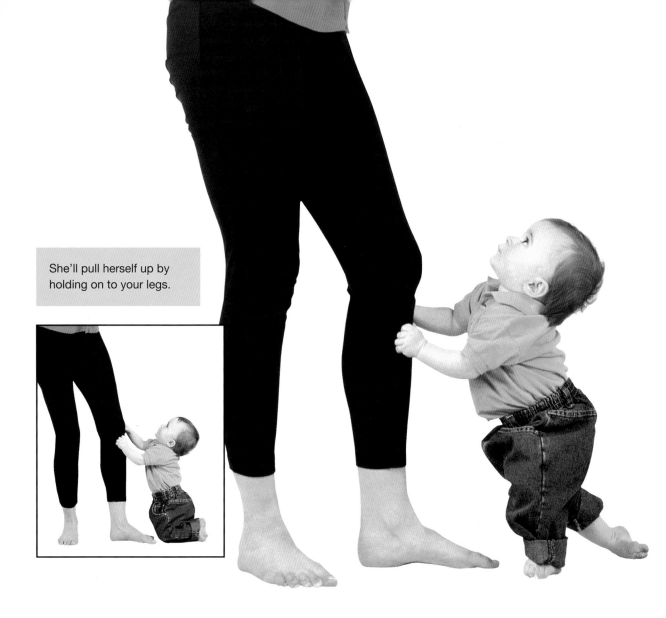

She'll pull herself up by holding on to your legs.

Up On Her Feet

Standing is another exciting achievement for your baby. There is
quite a wide variation in the age at which babies learn to stand on
their own. Most babies do it some time between nine and 15 months.

First, your baby will be able to take her own weight on her feet
provided you're holding her under her arms to steady her. Then she
will attempt to pull herself into a standing position using anything she
can get hold of - a table leg, the sides of her cot, or your legs. She'll
hang on, enjoying this new vantage point, then collapse. She will use
these props for support at first, and later on just to steady herself.

She'll be able to stand up for a while provided she's got something stable to hang on to, but getting down again may be more of a problem. At first you might have to come and help her sit down – several dozen times a day!

After a while she will start "cruising" round the furniture - walking sideways while holding on. Eventually she will find the confidence to let go and stand by herself. She'll collapse but she will keep on trying because she is so desperate to master this new skill. One day she will take her first few wobbly steps - and everyone will make a big fuss of her.

Re-arrange the furniture so she can hold on to it and walk sideways round the room.

How You Can Help

Put one of her favourite toys on the sofa or armchair to encourage her to pull herself up to reach it. Make sure your furniture is sturdy enough to take her weight. Remove anything she could pull over onto herself, such as a lightweight coffee table. And this is the time to do away with tablecloths.

Re-arrange the furniture, putting things close together so she can do a small circuit round the room, holding on. Have narrow gaps between the pieces of furniture at first - then, as she grows more confident, wider gaps.

Standing up, holding onto a large beach ball, is good for developing her sense of balance.

At first some babies tend to stand on tiptoe because of the excitement of it all. If your baby does, gently position her feet flat on the floor to teach her the right way to stand.

Teach her how to sit down again, by releasing her hands from whatever she's holding and gently lowering her bottom to the floor.

Let her walk barefoot - she doesn't need shoes until she's walking outside. If it's too cold for bare feet on hard floors, slipper socks with non-slip soles are a good idea.

Stand your baby between your legs, hold both her hands out at the sides, and walk together. She'll also enjoy walking along holding hands with an adult on each side.

If she is desperate to walk and hasn't quite managed it yet, this can be a frustrating time. If she seems more difficult than usual, won't lie down to have her nappy changed and refuses to co-operate when you're dressing her, that could be the reason why.

To encourage her, sit a few steps away, hold your arms out and play "walk to Daddy!" For those first steps, nothing beats the feeling of launching herself from one grown-up into the arms of another.

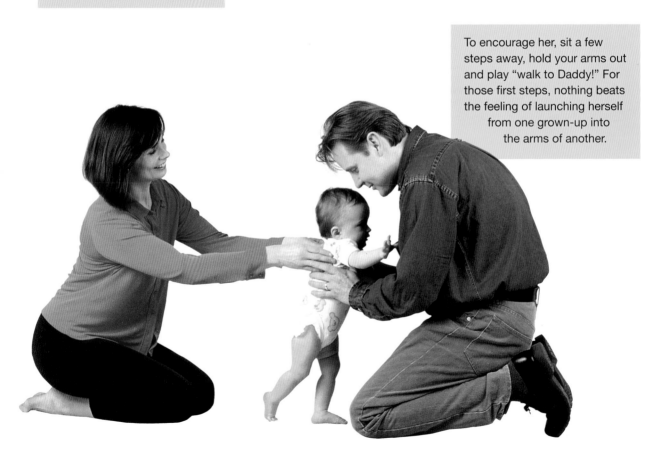

Early Or Late Walker?

Babies develop at different rates. Some babies learn to crawl and walk at a much earlier age than others. From nine to 16 months is the normal range for starting to walk, for instance. The timing is determined by a baby's muscle strength, her ability to balance and, perhaps most important, her personality - her motivation and confidence. A placid baby who is content to sit and play won't start walking as early as a more active baby who's keen to explore. Weight may also play a part, with heavier babies taking longer to get up on their feet. Encourage your baby, but don't try to rush her if she's not ready.

It's tempting to compare notes with other parents, but if your baby isn't doing the same things as other babies of her age, be patient - she'll get there in her own good time. Just try to enjoy each stage as it comes.

If you are worried that her development is delayed, talk to your health visitor about it.

A sturdy push-along toy will give her confidence. If the push-along trolley runs away from her, weigh it down with telephone directories.

Her developing hand skills open the way for new sorts of games and toys. Toys with buttons to press encourage your baby's increasing skill in using her index finger for prodding and poking.

Prodding, Pointing And Picking Up

Your baby is now using her hands in a different way. Instead of using her whole hand to pick up objects in her palm, she starts to use her thumb against several fingers and, by 12 months, her thumb and forefinger in a "pincer" grasp. This means she can pick up smaller things. She also starts to use her forefinger to point and to prod things, poking it into every little hole she can find.

When she reaches for an object she wants to take hold of, she adjusts the shape of her hand and the angle at which she approaches the object. This shows she is thinking about the object's shape and the best way to pick it up, rather than just plonking her hand on top of it and hoping for the best.

She also learns to let go of things on purpose - before, she would either drop a toy by accident or not know how to put it down. Until she develops this skill, she will find it easier to let go of something when there is a firm surface underneath it. You can help by letting her play at a small table or with her highchair tray in front of her, or by putting your open hand underneath the toy to encourage her to release it.

Once she has got the idea, she will delight in dropping toys for you to pick up and hand back to her so she can drop them again – she will want to play this game long after you are bored with it! When she's in her highchair, put a bucket or waste paper basket on the floor to one side of her, give her a pile of bricks and see if she can aim for the basket and get them in one by one.

"We used to have battles over the spoon when I was feeding her, but now I use two - she has one spoon that she can hold and play with, and I have another to actually get food into her mouth."

CLARE

She'll get a lot of satisfaction when she finds she can make exciting things happen by turning a knob or dial on an activity centre.

She puts things into her mouth for further exploration. Let her practise using her new pincer grasp on things that she can safely chew, like food - soft bits of banana and pasta or cooked vegetables, for example.

She may be more interested in mashing and smearing her food everywhere than actually eating it, and want to be more independent and in control at mealtimes. Resistance on your part is useless - but wrapping her in a large sleeved bib and putting a plastic sheet under the highchair might help you feel a little more relaxed about this "chimps' teaparty" phase!

You might be able to tell whether your baby is right- or left-handed. From around nine months onwards, offer her a toy in the middle of her body and see which hand she uses to take it. Try this several times and you could find she consistently prefers using one hand to the other. Offer the toy on the opposite side and see if she tends to reach across her body to take it with her preferred hand rather than the nearest hand. You might find she sucks on her less dominant hand, freeing up her favoured hand to use for exploring things. However, some children remain ambidextrous until they are 18 months or older.

Your baby can now give a toy to you as well as take it from you. At first, she will find it easier to let go of it if you put your hand underneath.

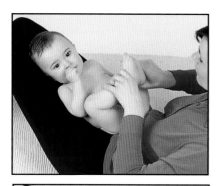

Baby Gymnastics

Babies are naturally wonderfully supple and it's good if they can stay that way as they grow. Here is a routine for a baby aged from around six to seven months onwards which will help keep her joints flexible by taking them through their full range of movement. The exercises will help to give her an understanding of what her body can and can't do, and will help build her physical confidence.

Clap her feet together and raise them up to her abdomen, then her chest.

With your baby lying on your knees, facing forwards, press each of her feet up towards her bottom, then try the same movement with both of her feet together.

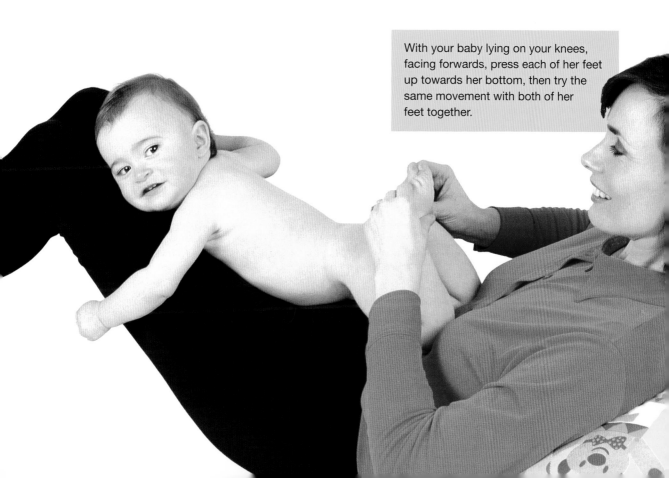

It's a good idea to have a "gymnastics" session like this when you are both in the mood and you have a few minutes to spare. Your baby will enjoy having your undivided attention. While you do these exercises, hold your baby securely, but don't press on her joints or bones. Aim for calm and smooth movements, not jerky ones. Your baby should be naked or in simple, loose clothing.

Holding her by the hips or legs, lift her legs up towards you so she does a shoulder stand, and kiss or blow on her feet to make her giggle.

Stretch her arms and shoulders. With your baby sitting on your lap facing forwards, gently bring her arms up above her head. Then open your baby's arms and bring them around your sides.

As well as these exercises, your baby will enjoy being waltzed around the room as you dance to music. Babies have a good sense of rhythm and when she can stand, she will start to "dance" when music comes on - it's a great party piece.

You'll find that you carry your baby differently now. Older babies can support their upper body, so you'll tend to carry her on your hip, with her legs wrapped round your waist. She'll also like to have piggyback rides or be hoisted up onto your shoulder for a new and exciting vantage point.

Lie on your back with your knees up, and let her lie flat on your lower legs. Hold her by the hands or around her chest.

Let her sit upright on your legs while you lightly support her with your hands around her chest. This will help develop her sense of balance - and it's fun, too!

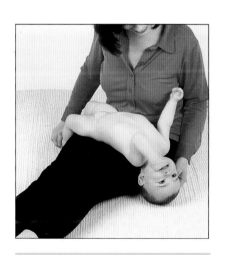

Lay her across your thighs in a backbend to gently stretch her spine.

Although she will enjoy rough and tumble play and can get around without you, there will still be times when your baby needs cuddles and quiet times with you, when you hold her close, rock her or sing to her. She will start to show you affection, hugging you in return.

Taking Your Baby Swimming

Taking your baby swimming from an early age gets her used to water and helps her feel at home in the pool, so it's good preparation for learning to swim later on.

You can take your baby swimming from around four months, when she has completed her injections, preferably in a special children's pool with warm water. Don't spend too long in the water - 10 to 15 minutes is long enough for young babies, as they get cold quickly. From around 12 months your baby might like to bob around in a baby swim-seat, which is like a swimming ring but also supports her from underneath.

Smile and talk to your baby to reassure her, and start by holding her close to you in the water or sitting on the steps so she can slowly get used to the idea. If she seems to be enjoying it, you can bob down in the water up to your shoulders, bounce her gently, support her while she "floats" and kicks, or play with a bath toy in the water. For more ideas, turn to page 85.

Now He's a Toddler

Your child has now discovered the delights of being able to toddle around for himself. Over the next few months he will invest all his energies into practising his new skill, becoming more and more agile and confident. He doesn't need you to bring him things. He can go out and explore the world for himself.

He will insist on freedom of movement, and will hate being restrained. Trying to keep him away from something he wants to explore will be a battle. He will also become more assertive and determined to do things his way.

Strangely, at the same time, he may drive you mad with his clinginess. He will go off on his own, but he will want to come back to you as his "base". A child who has just learned to walk is struggling with two powerful needs. He wants to see and touch and learn about everything, but at the same time, because so many experiences and events are new to him, he needs reassurance and can only feel secure enough to explore if he knows you are near.

A child's rate of physical growth slows down during the second year. Your toddler is likely to have less appetite

You have to learn to walk before you can run!

and he gradually loses his baby plumpness. He is on the go all the time. In the months after he has taken his first few steps, he will also learn other skills - to run, to sit himself down in a small chair, climb onto the sofa, go up the stairs on his hands and knees, walk sideways and backwards and throw things.

His desire to be independent will increase. Letting him learn to do things by himself will help him to develop a sense of accomplishment and confidence that will serve him well later when he goes to school. If your child is demanding to feed or dress himself or brush his own hair, try to cultivate a relaxed attitude, allow plenty of time and let him do it, even if it takes twice as long. Practising is the only way he will learn.

Good toys for this age are those that enable him to practise all his new-found skills and satisfy his need to explore and handle things. Now he's walking he will like trolleys and other toys that need to be pushed, sturdy sit-and-ride toys, and pull-

Thirteen-month-old Jedd enjoys pushing this train along. In a few months' time he will learn to walk backwards, pulling it towards him. Later on he will pull it behind him, confident that if he pulls the string it will follow.

alongs. He will love to drag and carry things around. He is constantly testing his own strength, seeing how big a box he can lift or how high he can climb.

He's Into Everything...

This is the stage when you wish
you had eyes in the back of your
head. Now your child can get around
so much faster and more easily, and he
has an insatiable curiosity and
seemingly limitless energy.

His urge to explore - opening every
drawer and cupboard, pressing every button, emptying every
waste paper basket and bookshelf - is very strong. Although it
may drive you to distraction, remind yourself that all he is
doing is practising and developing his new skills.

Your survival tactics will include childproofing your house
(see pages 51,58 and 78) and keeping a constant eye on your
toddler. He will get frustrated if there are too many things
around that he isn't allowed to investigate, so for your sanity
and his, move your valuables to another room or store them in a
cupboard with a childproof catch until this phase is over. There
are certain things that can't be moved out of his way, of course,
like the television or cooker. He has to be taught that he must
not touch them.

He won't just want to play with his own toys - he'll want
to use all the things that you use. You can help by giving him
objects or an area he can safely explore. For instance, have one
kitchen cupboard filled with unbreakable cups, bowls and

Toddlers have a great desire
for power. He will enjoy
anything that gives him a
feeling of being big and
important. Making a loud noise
– with drums, hammering toys
or anything else he can bang
with - makes him feel
powerful.

utensils in which he can sit and play to his heart's content.
Use the bottom shelf of the bookcase for his books, so you
won't mind if he pulls them all out.

Sitting him up with you at the dining table will be
fraught to begin with, because he will snatch at everything in
sight. If your baby does grab a knife or anything else that's
sharp, your first instinct will be to try to get hold of it and take
it out of his hand. This will just make him cling to it even
more tightly with the result that he may cut himself. Instead,
try squeezing his wrist - this will make him loosen his grip so
you can prise his fingers away and remove the object safely.

If emptying your handbag is a
source of fascination for him, let
him play with an old one that you
have filled with interesting - but
safe - bits and pieces.

Up And Over!

Many toddlers have a great urge to climb. They will scale everything they can, and get a wonderful feeling of satisfaction from ending up higher than when they started. The trouble is that climbing can also bring your child into conflict with you - and cause bumps on the head, or worse, for him, if it's not done safely. To make life easier on both of you, give a little thought to how you can help your toddler fulfil his need to climb without coming to grief.

He'll probably use the armchairs or sofa for his first attempts at climbing. Show him how to climb off safely, feet first. Decide which pieces of furniture are safe for him to climb on and which aren't, and start teaching him which ones he can use.

The stairs are another great challenge for an eager climber - but make sure you're right behind him. Until you are sure he can manage the stairs, carry on using the safety gates. But sooner or later he will need to learn how to go up and downstairs without falling. When you feel he is ready, show him how to do it safely. He should turn around at the top of the stairs, so he is facing the top, and come down backwards on his tummy, feet first.

⚠ Where Not To Climb

- He could hurt himself if he climbs out of his cot - lower the base before he learns how to do it.
- Always use a harness in his highchair or buggy, as these could tip over if he climbs while he is in them.
- If your toddler climbs onto dining chairs and leans over the back, disaster is sure to follow. It's safer for him to have a toddler-sized chair to sit on, and a toddler-sized table to play at, and he's likely to stay there and play for longer.

Get down on the floor with him and let him clamber over you, or get on your hands and knees and let him climb on your back.

Take him to a toddler group that has some big equipment for climbing - or buy something yourself for the garden. He might enjoy attending a toddler gym class which offers scope for climbing. Or you could take him to an indoor "soft" adventure playground. Most of these have areas with lots of lovely big shapes for little ones to scramble over. Some playgrounds have special areas with safe climbing equipment for the under-fives.

Walking outside on bumpy ground in the park or the woods will help him develop good balance.

Handy Work

Most of your child's play will involve using his hands in some way. Although some children become good at doing things with their hands at an earlier age than others, the development of hand skills follows a similar pattern in all children as they go through the same stages.

By around 15 months children can usually throw things, push toy cars along and build a tower two bricks high. They also learn to hold a crayon and scribble - see page 104 for how this develops into drawing and writing.

If you haven't already worked out whether your child is right- or left-handed, it should become clearer now.

At this stage he will happily oblige by going to get something you have asked him for. He is also learning the names of things, so play "fetching" games in which he has to go and find something in another room and bring it to you, or hide a toy (not too well!) and let him "find" it for you.

If he wants to help, make it easier for him by providing scaled-down tools for him to use, like this toddler-sized brush and dustpan.

"Sean is 13 months old and he started walking at 11 months. He's fairly confident now but he's still a bit unsteady and falls over quite a lot."

VANESSA

By around 18 months a child can push and pull large toys, he begins to turn the pages of a book one at a time, he can hold a cup and feed himself, take off his socks and shoes and turn a door handle.

His hand skills develop along with increased understanding. Your child can now play with toys that require some manipulation, and which also provide him with a mental challenge. You can see him planning his strategy before he acts.

Just watch his mind working as he plays with a stacking toy or containers that fit inside each other, deciding which one should go next.

As well as playing with toys that allow him to practise his manipulative skills, he will enjoy "helping" around the house in any way he can. Try to think of activities he can join in, such as wiping down the front of the fridge with a damp cloth, taking the shopping out of the bag or watering the plants in the garden.

Keeping all his toys in a toybox will encourage him to fling them out onto the floor. If there are too many toys around, it's difficult for him to decide which to choose. Try to keep just a few toys out on low shelves or surfaces, so he can easily see what is there and decide what he wants to play with. Every so often, change the toys that you keep out, so he doesn't get bored with them.

> ⚠ **Keep Him Safe**
>
> - **Now that he can turn screwtops, keep household chemicals, medicines and alcohol locked away out of sight**
> - **If you have glass at low levels in your home, replace it with special safety glass or stick safety film over it.**

His mental skills and his hand skills improve in tandem. Playing with a shape sorter requires some thought, as well as the ability to put the shapes in the holes.

A Toddler Workout

Here's a mini-workout to do together from around 12 months onwards. It will help your child's flexibility, strength and balance. Try it when you have a few minutes to spare. Only do the exercises your child enjoys.

A rhyme for bending and stretching your arms high up in the air is: "Clap your hands, one, two, three, put your hands upon your knees. Lift them high to touch the sky, clap, clap hands and away they fly!"

Start by encouraging him to stretch out his arms and shoulders. Think of rhymes that will get him stretching and make it fun at the same time. For instance, get him to stretch his arms out to the sides as you both do the actions to: "Baby's shoes, Mummy's shoes, Daddy's shoes, Giant's shoes." Your arms should get wider as you demonstrate the size of each shoe, until they are fully outstretched as you shout out "Giant's shoes!"

"Baby's shoes,
Mummy's shoes,
Daddy's shoes,
Giant's shoes.!"

A child develops control over his body from the middle outwards - his shoulders and elbows before his wrists and fingers, and his hips and knees before his ankles and feet. Help him develop an awareness of his ankles, and what they can do, by "winding" his feet in circular movements while he sits on the floor with his legs apart.

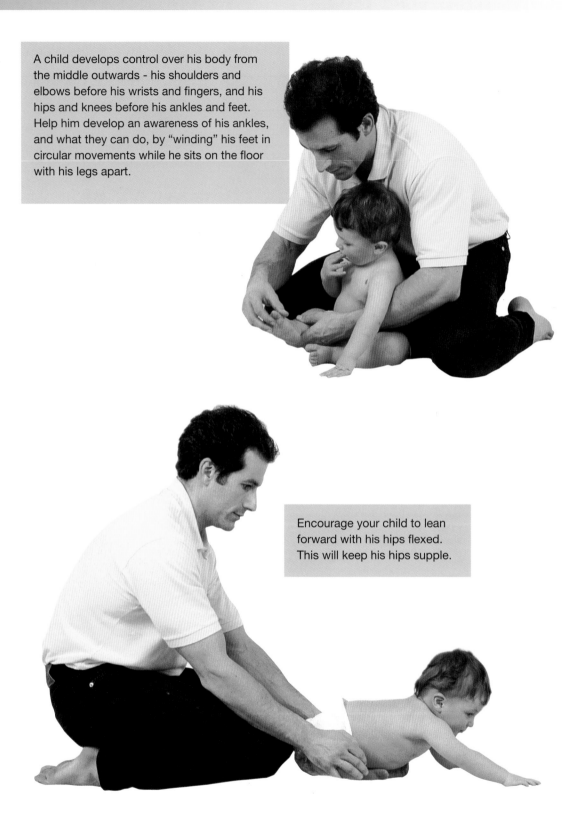

Encourage your child to lean forward with his hips flexed. This will keep his hips supple.

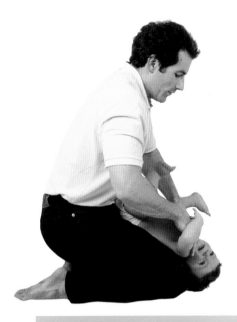

1 Kneel, with your child on your legs facing you.

2 Lift him up by the hips so he is standing on his shoulders. If he's happy with that, lift him up higher.

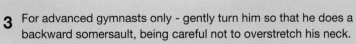

3 For advanced gymnasts only - gently turn him so that he does a backward somersault, being careful not to overstretch his neck.

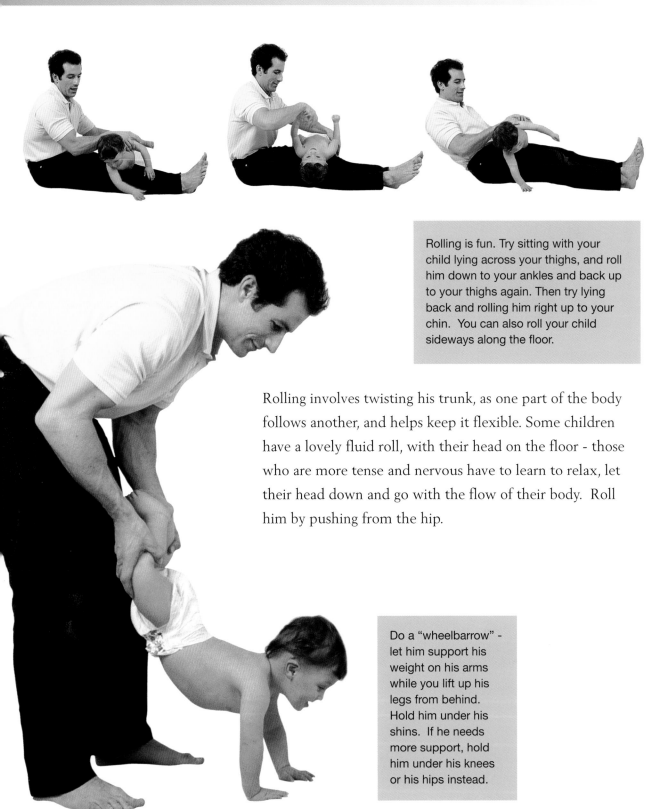

Rolling is fun. Try sitting with your child lying across your thighs, and roll him down to your ankles and back up to your thighs again. Then try lying back and rolling him right up to your chin. You can also roll your child sideways along the floor.

Rolling involves twisting his trunk, as one part of the body follows another, and helps keep it flexible. Some children have a lovely fluid roll, with their head on the floor - those who are more tense and nervous have to learn to relax, let their head down and go with the flow of their body. Roll him by pushing from the hip.

Do a "wheelbarrow" - let him support his weight on his arms while you lift up his legs from behind. Hold him under his shins. If he needs more support, hold him under his knees or his hips instead.

Let's Play!

At this age, your child's developing sense of humour means you can really make him giggle. He'll love it when you tickle him or have some rough and tumble play together. With some children the more you man-handle them the better they like it, while others are a bit more cautious. Let your child set the pace and watch out for signals that say you've gone far enough.

This kind of physical play is good for a child. The sensations he gets when he learns to move in different ways with your help - balancing, flying through the air, sliding, being rolled over - all help him to realize what his body can do. He learns to feel secure with you, to trust you not to drop him or let him get hurt. It helps to use up some of his excess energy – and it's exciting and exhilarating!

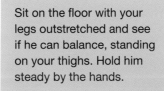

Sit on the floor with your legs outstretched and see if he can balance, standing on your thighs. Hold him steady by the hands.

Here are some ideas:

- Make a tunnel with your body by getting down on all fours, and let him escape by crawling out through your arms, between your legs, or at the sides.

- "Throw" him in the air or onto the sofa (counting "one, two, three..." before you launch him adds to the suspense).

- Hoist him up above your head, then tip him down between your legs, and swing him back up in the air again.

- Don't forget the "Ring a ring o'roses" rhyme.

- Take turns at rolling each other along the floor - even if you have to do most of the movement yourself, let him think he managed to roll you.

- Sit on the floor and hold him against your body quite tightly, enclosed within a "prison" of your legs and arms - he has to try to escape.

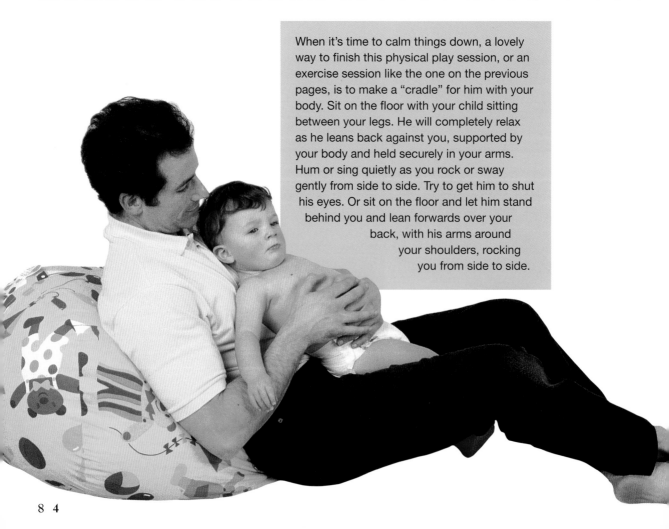

When it's time to calm things down, a lovely way to finish this physical play session, or an exercise session like the one on the previous pages, is to make a "cradle" for him with your body. Sit on the floor with your child sitting between your legs. He will completely relax as he leans back against you, supported by your body and held securely in your arms. Hum or sing quietly as you rock or sway gently from side to side. Try to get him to shut his eyes. Or sit on the floor and let him stand behind you and lean forwards over your back, with his arms around your shoulders, rocking you from side to side.

Come On In, The Water's Lovely!

If your child has been going to the swimming pool regularly from an early age and is confident in the water, you can be a little more adventurous now.

Encourage him to kick and splash with his feet while he holds onto the side of the pool. When he's got the idea, tow him along by the arms while he kicks out behind him. Then support him in the water, under his chest, and get him to use his arms and legs for doggy paddle. Don't worry too much about teaching him the proper strokes at this stage. If he enjoys the water and isn't afraid to get his face wet he's doing well.

See if he can lie back and relax in the water, making his body into a star shape, while you support him with your hands under his back and bottom. If he uses armbands, it's a good idea to spend some time in the water without them each time you go swimming, so he can get used to how it feels.

Play games like "Ring a ring o'roses", where you both duck down in the water for a second. Try blowing bubbles in the water. If you're allowed to take a beach ball into the pool with you, you can both chase it around in the water. Encourage him to stand on the side and leap into your arms.

"Look What I Can Do"

O nce a toddler has been walking for six months or so, he will progress to running - and won't trip up so much. He is also more aware of obstacles and can weave in and out as he runs. He will learn to walk backwards, and on tiptoe.

He will get better at going upstairs - first he will need to hold on and will go up one step at a time, putting both feet on each step. By the age of around two you'll probably feel you can trust him on the stairs. He will start to jump - taking off with both feet - and will delight in jumping off a step over and over again. He may also be pedalling around on a tricycle. He can bounce on a trampoline and use a slide. He will be able to throw a ball overhand and kick a large ball on the ground. He can turn one page at a time when he looks at a book. He will start scribbling with crayons on paper. He will be able to do simple inset puzzles and thread large beads on a string. Having gone through the various stages of pulling things apart and emptying containers, your child now spends long periods investigating various ways of building things up, stacking them, putting them together and rearranging them.

Milo, who is two and a half, can balance on one foot for a couple of seconds. He is very proud when he manages to do something new.

Learning to speak is a big step forward. He relies less on body language, and is learning to express his feelings and ask for what he wants.

His mental development is making huge strides too. He can now understand more, remember events and places, and work some things out for himself. He will know, for instance, that when the doorbell rings it means there's someone at the front door.

He'll need you to play with him and give him lots of practice with his new skills.

He likes putting things together at this stage. Building towers is nearly as much fun as knocking them down!

Gradually he learns to do more and more for himself - and if he wants your help, he'll let you know. He will be very determined and assertive. Getting a toddler at the "terrible twos" stage to co-operate with you will demand all your ingenuity and the patience of a saint. There's certainly never a dull moment.

Start with a great big stretch, as high and as wide as you can go - then curl up very small, in a tight little ball.

- Open your fingers as wide as you can, then clench your fists tight.

- Stretch one arm out in front of you for a few seconds while holding the other behind your back, then quickly change them over, and change them over again. Do it faster and faster.

Music And Movement

If you're lucky there might be music and dance classes for young children near where you live - ask around among your friends, or at the local library. If there is not, here are some ideas to try out at home. Tailor these suggestions to your child's abilities and understanding, and add your own special favourites - and your child's. Do the exercises along with him, and repeat each movement several times if he is enjoying it. Music adds to the fun. You can also buy cassettes of children's songs to give you more inspiration. It's more fun with other people - why not invite some friends round to join in?

With your arms held out to the sides, sway from side to side, putting your weight first on one leg and then on the other.

- Stretch up on tiptoes, then squat down, and jump up high again. Shake out each of your legs in turn. Shake out your shoulders and arms and let your whole body go wobbly like a jelly.

- Get your child to crouch down and be a jack-in-the-box. Wind him up by "turning a key" in his back, so he will jump up.

Use your hands and arms to imitate different animal movements. Here are a few to try, but make up some of your own as well. To make a fish swimming through the water, put your palms together and move your hands at the wrists. A snake can be suggested by one writhing arm. Make a snapping crocodile's jaws by placing your elbows together and clapping one hand on top of the other.

• On your feet again, do different walking styles - on tiptoes, or huge strides, stamping or marching.

• Get your child to experiment with using his body to make different shapes. Show him how to make himself as small as a mouse, as tall as a house, as wide as a bridge and as flat as a pancake.

• Experiment with different styles of movement - going around the room like a bear, on hands and feet, lumbering like an elephant waving its "trunk" (one arm in front of your face); or be a happy puppy on all fours, wagging its "tail".

Sit with your legs stretched out in front of you. Alternately flex and point your feet. Bend your knee and, with your ankle resting on your thigh, rotate your foot. Repeat with the other leg.

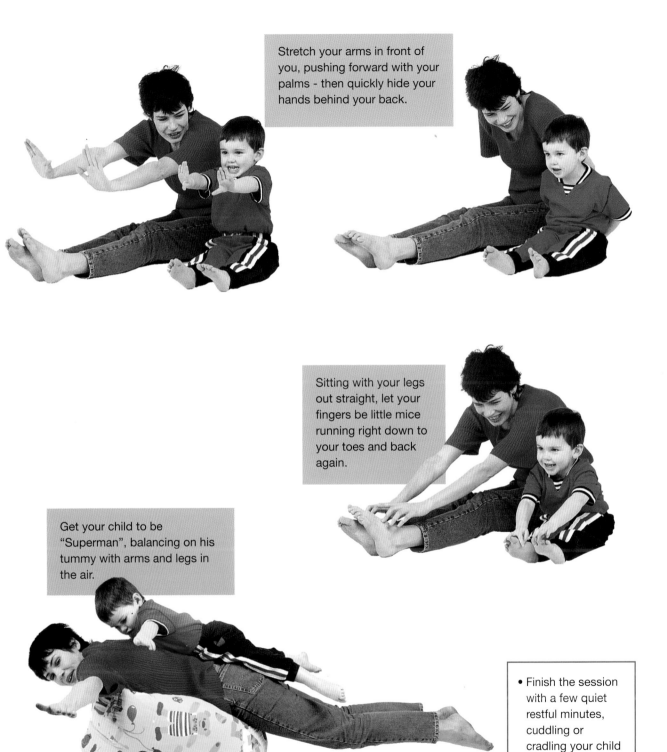

Stretch your arms in front of you, pushing forward with your palms - then quickly hide your hands behind your back.

Sitting with your legs out straight, let your fingers be little mice running right down to your toes and back again.

Get your child to be "Superman", balancing on his tummy with arms and legs in the air.

• Finish the session with a few quiet restful minutes, cuddling or cradling your child (see page 84).

"The elephant walks

    (Sway from side to side with legs apart)

Like this and that

He's terribly tall

    (Indicate how tall and fat by stretching

    your arms)

And terribly fat

He's got no fingers

    (Wiggle your fingers)

He's got no toes

    (Point to or wiggle your toes)

But goodness gracious

    (Make a trunk with your arm in front of

    your nose)

What a nose!"

Games, Songs And Rhymes

Children start responding to rhythm from an early age. Put a tape or CD on and boogie round the room together. Try dancing in different styles - show your child your idea of happy, sad, fierce or silly dancing and encourage him to try. Or have a musical bumps session - when you turn the music down he has to sit down straight away. In musical statues, he has to stop and stand very still when the music stops.

    Another game that children love - which goes down well at parties - is for you to blow bubbles just above their heads and they have to reach up and clap the bubbles to pop them.

    Your child will enjoy all the old favourite songs and nursery rhymes. They will give him an appreciation of the sound of words and rhymes which will stand him in good stead when it is time to learn to read. If you feel silly singing or you

"Heads and shoulders, knees and toes, knees and toes
Heads and shoulders, knees and toes, knees and toes
Eyes and ears and mouth and nose
Heads and shoulders, knees and toes!"
(Touch each part of the body with both hands as you sing its name.)

can't remember how the songs go, invest in a good book, a CD or cassette.

Here are a few ideas.

Don't forget "Here we go round the mulberry bush", the 'Hokey Cokey', "Incy wincy spider" and "One, two, buckle my shoe" !

> **"I'm a little teapot, short and stout**
> (Bend your knees and make a circle to show how fat you are)
> **Here's my handle**
> (Put your right hand on your hip)
> **Here's my spout**
> (Left arm up in spout shape)
> **When I get the steam up, hear me shout**
> **'Tip me up and pour me out!' "**
> (Tilt to the left as if pouring from the spout)

> **"Row, row, row your boat**
> **Gently down the stream**
> **Merrily, merrily, merrily, merrily**
> **Life is but a dream..."**

"This is the way the ladies ride, 'trit-trot, trit-trot, trit-trot'
This is the way the gentlemen ride, 'a-gallop, a-gallop, a-gallop'
This is the way the farmers ride,
'hobbledy-hoy, hobbledy-hoy'
And DOWN, into the ditch!"
(This ride gets faster and more furious with each successive line, ending up with your child "falling off" the horse.)

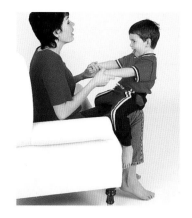

Here's another traditional "tipping off the lap" song:
"I took my girl to a ball last night
I took her to a supper
The table broke and she fell down
And dipped her nose in the butter"

Your child will probably learn this next one at playgroup:
"The wheels on the bus go round and round
Round and round, round and round
The wheels on the bus go round and round
All day long"

Do the actions to as many verses as you know, including "the doors on the bus they open and close", "the horn on the bus goes beep, beep, beep", "the wipers on the bus go swish, swish,swish", "the people on the bus bounce up and down", "the babies on the bus go 'Waah, waah, waah!' " and "the ladies on the bus go chatter, chatter, chatter".

Amazing Acrobatic Feats

It's always a good idea to warm up before any strenuous physical activity session - it loosens you up, slowly stretches your muscles and gets them ready for more vigorous exercise. Stretching up with your whole body, circling your arms and shoulders, marching, dancing and skipping are good ways to warm up. End each session by stretching out, cooling down and relaxing.

Here are some physical games and stunts your child might enjoy.

Lie on your front and let your child sit astride your back. Bump him up and down and, if he likes that, get up onto your hands and knees while he clings on with his arms around your neck and grips with his legs round your waist. You can sway to and fro or from side to side and - if you can trust him to hold on - give him a ride round the room.

Balancing

He will love to perform feats of balance to an admiring audience. For his first trick, he can try to balance on you - sit on the floor with your knees bent and see if he can stand up on your knees, holding your hands to steady himself. This takes a lot of concentration.

Stretch a "tightrope" along the floor and get your child to try to keep each foot on the rope as he walks along it. Stretching his arms out to the sides will help him balance.

Find other things for your child to balance on, like a length of shelving resting on telephone directories at each end. Walking on walls outside is always a big favourite. If you encourage him to hold your fingertip rather than hanging onto your hand, this will help him to find his own balance.

Jumping

Jumping on stepping stones around the room is a good game, especially to music. Put down several "stepping stones" - anything that won't slide about is suitable, such as table mats or cushions. He has to go around the room by striding or jumping from one to the other, without touching the carpet, which is shark-infested water.

From the age of around two and a half, your child will be able to jump with two feet. He can practise this new skill by jumping down from a step, or the bottom stair, or jumping to something on the floor - like the skipping rope or a table mat.

Help him to do a really big jump up in the air by holding his hands or elbows. If there are two of you, you can support him by holding him under the elbows and holding his hands, and launch him so that you turn his jump into a flying leap through the air.

• Hold one handle of the skipping rope and shake it to make the rope into a wiggly snake for your child to jump over.

Sliding

If you have a slippery floor, take your child by the calves and slide him along the floor, or make big sweeping movements from side to side so that his body bends at the waist. Try sitting back to back and slide him along the floor by pushing backwards as you "walk" with your hands and feet.

Lie on your back with your knees bent up to your chest, and let your child try to keep his balance as he sits astride your legs. Bounce him up and down as you sing "Rock-a-bye baby on the tree top." When you get to "Down will come cradle, baby and all", tip him off (gently) as you roll to one side. Make sure he has a soft landing. (To make this easier on your back you could lie on the bed or on some cushions. Take care not to arch your back - keep it flat.)

How Strong Can He Be?

Get your child to sit on the floor, with his knees bent and feet apart and his hands on the floor. The idea is that he stays as steady as a rock while you push him from different angles. Tell him you are going to try to push him over, but don't actually do it - let him experience the feeling of strength and firmness as he braces himself against your hands. Then swap roles and let him try to push you over. (And who knows, if he tries with all his strength, this time it might just be possible.)

Another way of letting your child experience his own strength is to get him to lie on his side and curl up into a very tight ball, hugging his knees, while you pull gently on each arm and leg in turn, trying to prise them away from the centre of his body. He resists, and you find (don't you) that he is too strong for you - you just can't do it, however hard you try.

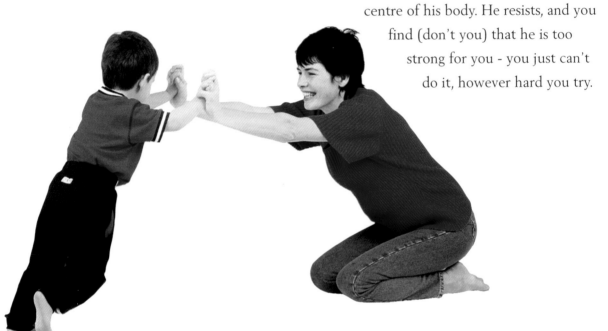

Energetic Games

As well as throwing and catching a ball, he might enjoy knocking skittles over, throwing the ball to you through a hoop, playing football and pouncing on a rolling ball like a goalie.

Chasing games are always fun - especially if there are two adults around so he can run from one "scary" grown-up to the other "safe" one.

Out And About

A walk outside can be a wonderful experience for a young child. There are so many fascinating things to look at - cars, lorries, dogs, trees, leaves, ducks, the milkman, the shops, the puddles on the pavement. It also offers a chance to use his new skill - running as fast and as far as he can.

Once he starts to get up a bit of speed, he'll find your flat or house and garden too constricting. At the sight of a stretch of pavement or a long supermarket aisle he'll be off like a rocket, so try to go out regularly to somewhere he can run safely to his heart's content.

A walk to the park might seem like a good idea, but under-threes are not very good at walking alongside you. They find it hard to walk from A to B, and can't walk purposefully with an adult for long. Their natural tendency is to dart around rather than walk in a straight line. They use you as a secure base and will gravitate around you if you stay in one place. If you're moving, they can't do this.

Sometimes you'll be able to take the time to go for a walk at your child's pace and stand by as he explores all the doorways and steps along the street. But if you've decided what you really want is to spend an hour in the park, it might make life easier and less frustrating for both of you if you take him in the buggy and then let him get out and walk around when you're there. Taking the buggy also means you won't end up with a child who wants you to carry him when it's time to go home.

When a child won't walk with you and keeps lifting up his arms to be carried, telling him to hurry up, or walking away in the hope that he will walk after you, only makes matters worse. He knows that once you move off he won't be able to stay close to you. So, let him ride to and from wherever you're going and give him the freedom to get out of the buggy when you get there.

Keeping Him On A Tight Rein

Letting your child walk outside near roads or in busy shopping centres can be a fraught business at this stage, which is why many mothers use reins on their toddlers. A pair of reins prevents him making a bolt for freedom as soon as he gets out of the door, and also lets you stop him from falling if he's still a bit unsteady on his feet.

Holding your hand means he has to hold his arm up high above his head which can get tiring; he will try to yank you in every direction and he can also squirm out of your grip and dart off. Reins are more comfortable as well as safer than holding hands. He may not like them - but if you want him to wear them, persevere until he accepts the inevitable.

"Todd is nearly three. He loves his sandpit and will play happily for ages. He also likes making model spaceships by gluing boxes together."

MANDY

Time For Playgroup

As your child approaches the age of three, you will probably want him to go to pre-school or playgroup. There are lots of benefits to be had by attending a good playgroup. He learns to get along with other children, to share and take turns, he gets used to new adults and learns to listen and follow instructions - all good preparation for starting school.

There will be a wide range of activities for him to choose from. As well as helping him socially and educationally, playgroup or nursery gives him the chance to try out physical activities and challenges that might not be possible at home.

There might be some large equipment such as a slide or climbing frame, a tunnel, large blocks or balance beams, and toys such as scooters, tricycles and hoops. There may be music and movement sessions in a large group with the other children.

He'll have the opportunity to try out all sorts of games and activities that will improve his manipulative skills, such as peg boards, lacing and threading sets and construction toys as well as cutting, sticking and collage.

There will also be scope for more frequent and large-scale messy play with sand, water and paint than you can bear to put up with at home!

Most playgroups provide some outdoor play space too, but if they don't then the leaders will probably take the children on regular outings instead.

The Pre-School Learning Alliance recommends that every playgroup session should include:

- A balance of large and small muscle activities to develop physical skills.

- A variety of interactions with adults and other children to develop social and language skills.

- A variety of challenging experiences to develop intellectual ability.

- A range of natural materials to develop creative skills - such as sand, water, clay, dough and fabrics.

- Varied opportunities for imaginative play and exploration to encourage personal and emotional development.

- Opportunities to learn to respect and value all people.

If your child goes to a children's gym class such as Tumble Tots (see page 127 in Chapter 7), he will have the chance to use equipment to hang, bounce, jump and slide. He will become more and more confident, while learning his physical limitations. A trip to Tumble Tots or the gym class is a good way to channel some of his energy in a constructive way.

Some children prefer a less structured approach. If your child is like this, he might enjoy a regular trip to an indoor adventure playground. These "soft play" centres provide plenty of scope for active children, with equipment such as ladders, nets, ball-ponds, slides and big foam shapes so little ones can throw themselves around as much as they like. Most of these indoor adventure playgrounds have a special section set aside where younger children can play safely away from the fray.

Keep Fit, Have Fun

What She Can Do Now

At the age of around three your child will be able to go upstairs like an adult, on alternating feet, though she may still come down two feet to a step. She can pedal and steer a tricycle. She can use scissors and enjoys cutting and gluing pictures. She can catch a ball with two hands. She can use a fork and spoon well and can dress herself, apart from tying her shoelaces.

At four, she can balance on one foot for several seconds, and can hop forwards on her dominant foot. She goes up and down stairs on alternate feet. She can now handle small objects with even greater precision, and her drawings are becoming more detailed and accurate. She can catch, throw and kick a ball quite well.

At three and a half, Lily has good balance.

As far as hand skills go, your child will continue to develop new finger movements up to the age of about five, and from then on she will continually practise and improve the quality of these movements. She can copy short sequences of simple shapes or letters although she may copy them the wrong way round, and she can cut around simple shapes.

Although you will now be able to tell whether she is left- or right-handed, children tend to use both hands more than adults do, particularly if they are left-handed.

Starting To Draw And Write

A small child's first attempts at drawing are done simply for the pleasure of making a mark on something – smearing food on the highchair tray, for instance! At first she is not concerned with trying to draw a picture, she simply enjoys the experience of making lines and scribbles appear on paper - or the living-room wall! When your child is around 15 or 16 months, get out some chunky crayons and paper from time to time and see if she is ready to have a go with your help. (You may have to teach her not to put the crayons in her mouth.)

If you encourage your child's early scribbling and give her plenty of opportunity to practise, you will notice some changes over time as she gradually develops more control over the marks she makes.

All young children go through the same stages. They start by scribbling straight lines, then experiment with curves, circles, spirals, ovals and dots, and will repeat patterns and shapes and try new ones. From the age of around two and a half, they start to draw radiating lines (the sun) and combinations of circles and crosses.

Gradually, out of these shapes, the symbols for drawing people emerge. Her early drawings of people are likely to have a large circle for a head, with lines coming out of it for arms and legs. Eventually she will start to add the details. If there is something she has particularly noticed about a person, such as curly hair, that will be an important feature. She will also work out a formula for drawing other things around her, such as trees, houses, animals, flowers. How well her drawing develops from these early stages will partly depend on the opportunities she is given.

The best way to help your child is to be interested in what she is drawing. Ask if she'd like to tell you about her drawing.

Let her draw things in her own way, as she sees them, and praise her efforts.

Give her plenty of opportunity and materials for drawing. With small pieces of paper and only one or two colours she won't be able to achieve much artistically, so be prepared to provide her with a limitless supply of large sheets of paper and dozens of chunky crayons in different colours so her creativity can really start to flow! Let her experiment with different kinds of pens, pencils and crayons.

Paper can be expensive to buy. A cheaper alternative is to buy odd rolls of wallpaper and cut large pieces off them. Better still, you may know someone who can pass on unwanted or partially used stationery such as computer printouts.

Children often get frustrated when the paper moves around while they are trying to draw, before they have mastered the skill of holding it still with one hand while drawing with the other. Fix the sheet of paper to the table with bits of sticky tape or weight the corners.

As well as drawing she may enjoy painting, fingerpainting and printing with sponge shapes dipped in paint. Let her go out in the garden and make marks with coloured chalks on some paving. Through scribbling, your child learns how to control the crayon and make different kinds of marks by pulling and pushing and varying the pressure. This is the first exploratory step towards learning to write.

In time your child will pretend to write - she will produce lines of squiggles. Eventually she will try to write actual letters. Children are taught to write lower case letters at pre-school, but they see plenty of examples of capital letters in print around them on magazines, food packets and so on, and often their first spontaneous attempts at writing are strings of unrelated capital letters.

How Children Play

Play is essential for young children - it's not just fun, it's their way of learning about the world, of understanding how things work, of exploring who they are and what they can do. Your child will play in lots of different ways - and you can help.

Fantasy Play

Your child makes up stories and acts them out with dolls, animals or other little figures, or pretends to be someone else. The first sign of this will probably be when she pretends to feed a doll or imitates an animal. As her language skills and imagination develop, you will be amazed at what she comes out with.

You can help your child's pretend play by providing simple dressing up clothes and "props" like an upturned table and a blanket to cover its legs - to be a tent or a cave - or covers for Teddy's bed. You may be required to play various roles too.

Constructive Play

She builds with bricks, Lego, or other construction toys or piles boxes one on top of the other. You can help by encouraging her, helping when she wants you to, praising her efforts and giving her lots of different things to build with.

Social Play

This means playing games with other children, including party games and board games. Toddlers tend to play alongside other children rather than with them. It isn't until a child reaches the age of around three that she starts to play co-operatively with other children. Up to this time sharing and taking turns are concepts she simply won't understand - though she may share to please you if you tell her to. As she gets older, she gradually becomes aware that the world doesn't revolve around her and is more able to identify with other people's feelings.

Skilful play

Your child learns to use her hands and brain for finely controlled, small movements or complex sequences of activity - jigsaw puzzles, sorting, or threading beads.

"Both of my children, aged three and four, love rigging up a camp with an old blanket over the furniture, and playing in it with their torches."

JON

Energetic Play

Rough and tumble, running, climbing, jumping, balancing, swinging, playing outside and developing new physical skills - play like this is the main subject of this book, and hopefully you now have lots of ideas.

Exploratory Play

This means learning by discovery or by exploring everyday objects and materials, such as squeezy bottles, sand and water. To help, provide plenty of opportunities for your child to see, hear, touch and taste new things, and share her fascination and pleasure in discovering the different properties of various materials and objects.

Schemas

Experts in child psychology have identified what they call "schemas" in children's play. These are repeatable patterns of behaviour which are particularly evident in children from two to five.

Some easily identifiable schemas are connection (joining things up), enveloping (wrapping things up), enclosing (putting things inside other things), rotation (making things - or yourself - turn round and round), trajectory (making things move through the air, jumping or kicking) and transportation (moving things from one place to another).

"Rosie loves wrapping things up - writing little letters and putting them in envelopes. She is also very keen on folding up clothes and pillowcases!"

AMANDA

Children who have a strong inclination towards "connecting" will enjoy playing with construction toys, bricks or beads that interlock, joining up tracks for toy trains, and attaching trains and carriages together.

"Trajectory" children will spend a lot of their time throwing or kicking things, jumping from heights and riding round on bikes.

Children who are into "enveloping" will play at wrapping things up, making dens, putting things in the "oven", for example.

"Transportation" children may love to shift the furniture around or spend a lot of time moving all their dolls and cars from one place to another.

Girls often show more enclosing and enveloping schemas, while boys tend to be more trajectory.

Understanding about schemas gives you some insight into the way your child's mind works and helps you to accept her need to play in a certain way. If she's into trajectory play, for example, you'll have a hard job on your hands to get her to sit quietly and play with a construction toy - she's more likely to want to throw the bricks or make towers and knock them down than fit them together. The secret is to find ways she can play which will satisfy her needs. Find her games that involve trajectory play, like hammering and throwing games where she throws a bean-bag into a bucket.

Children need encouragement and the opportunity to experience all the different types of play but you also need to recognize and accommodate what interests them most.

A child who wants to play at dolls' teaparties all the time, for instance, could be encouraged to paint pictures to show what's on the menu at the dolls' cafe.

Time To Play

Children don't need expensive toys in order to play. They need to spend time with you and watch you and talk to you about everything from the washing up to what you are cooking for tea. Your child will love to look at books with you, learn nursery rhymes, sing songs and, of course, ask you questions about everything under the sun.

Sometimes she will need you to play with her so she can get the most out of a game or toy; at other times she will be happy to play by herself. In fact, quite often children need time to play alone or with their friends, to lose themselves in their own little world and make up their own imaginative games without any input from adults.

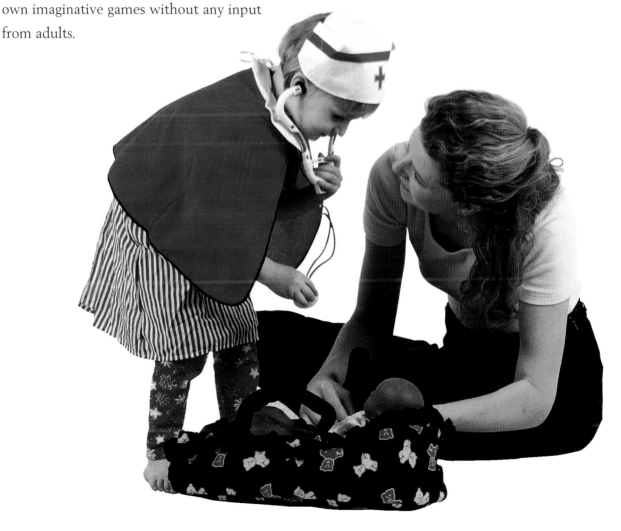

Let's Get Moving

When children reach the age of around four, they sometimes become less physically active, compared with younger children who are on the go all the time for the sheer joy of moving. They become more interested in things that involve sitting down - drawing, cutting and sticking, games and, of course, television and videos.

If your little couch potato needs some encouragement to get physical, the following activity session will introduce some fun and movement into her day. Even a boisterous child who's always active will benefit. Working on specific exercises, stretches and stunts like these is more constructive for her than running wildly around the house and flinging herself against the sofa or walls. If you can get her interested, it gives her something to aim for and a sense of achievement when she manages something new.

Stand with feet wide apart, then bend over from the waist and put your hands on the floor. Get your child to pull a funny face at you through her legs.

- Encourage your child, but don't push her to do anything she feels unsure about.

- Don't feel you have to do all of these exercises or do them in this order - just choose the ones that appeal.

- Remember to warm up first (page 95). Don't end your session too suddenly - finish with some of the gentler exercises so your heartbeat and breathing can slowly return to normal.

- Enjoyment - for both of you - should be the main aim.

Once she has had the opportunity to express her excess energy, your little whirlwind might be better able to sit down and concentrate on a more sedate activity for a while.

These exercises will help your child to think about how she is using her body. Even those children who have good skills at running, jumping and climbing need to develop what's called "spatial awareness" - a sense of where the different parts of their body are in relation to the space around them. Exercises and games like these help a child's "motor planning" - for instance when she is faced with something that's quite difficult to climb over, she has to work out what she needs to do to get over it and where she is able to move her arms and legs. And, of course, apart from anything else, the exercises are a fun way of playing together. Here we go!

Sit with your back straight, your knees to the sides and your feet in the centre (the tailor position) and gently bounce your knees up and down. Then stretch your feet out in front and "draw circles" by rotating your feet. Flex your feet backwards and forwards a few times. Call pointed toes "good toes", flexed toes "naughty toes".

Crouch down and let your child climb onto your back and balance there with her arms and legs stretched out in the shape of an aeroplane. If she's wobbly, hold her steady with your hands behind you.

- Kneel on the floor. Rotate your head so that you are "drawing" a big circle with the top of your head. Do this a couple of times, then go back the other way. Circle your shoulders - forwards a couple of times, then backwards a couple of times.

- Stand straight with your legs slightly apart. Starting with your arms stretched above your head, draw big circles in the air with your outstretched arms by swinging your body round from the waist. Pretend you're a windmill. Go round first one way, then the other.

"Since Sophie was three I've noticed a change in her - she has become much more confident and independent on the play equipment at the park. She wants to go on everything now."

SUE

You lie on your back with your legs bent. Your child leans with her tummy against the soles of your feet, and you slowly hoist her up in the air with your legs, holding her hands to support her. To protect your back, keep the small of your back flat against the floor - don't arch it.

Here's one for a daring acrobat. Face your child, standing with your knees slightly bent and your feet apart.
- Hold her hands or hold her under her arms as she climbs up, one foot on each of your thighs.
- Then both of you lean back and wait for the applause! For an encore, let her "walk" her feet up your thighs.
- Then, as you hold her hands, she performs a backwards somersault with her legs going up and over her head.

- Stand with your legs slightly apart, knees slightly bent. Put your hands on your hips and rotate your pelvis like a belly dancer.

- Squat down on your toes and jump up like a frog. Have a frogs' jumping race.

Give her a "bumpy ride" - lie on your back with your legs bent and your feet flat on the floor. Your child sits facing you, astride your pelvis. Hold your fingers up in front of her and let her choose one. When she has touched the finger of her choice, you start the ride by bouncing her up and down or swaying. Each finger gives her a different kind of ride - some are fast and furious, others are slow and smooth.

Now shake out your arms and legs and go all floppy like a rag doll. Bend over at the waist and let your arms dangle. Then slowly come back up to standing.

To finish with a restful stretch, get onto all fours and let your bottom drop down onto your feet. Stretch your arms out in front of you and let your head rest on the floor. Take your fingers as far forward as they will comfortably go as you stretch, then relax.

Fun And Games

Here are some more ideas for physical games and play that your child will enjoy.

• Get your child to move in as many different ways as you can think of - for instance, she could gallop or trot like a horse; run, jump, hop, skip, roll, jump like a frog; crawl; walk on tiptoes; walk on her knees; and shuffle or spin on her bottom. You could play a game where she has to do something different every time you clap your hands.

• Rolling together is fun. Lying stretched out on the floor, you put your arms around each other's bodies and then slowly roll over and over, staying together - when you're on top, don't rest your full weight on her in case you squash her.

• Teach her to play "Cat's got the measles". Face each other. Start by standing with your legs apart. Jump so that you end up with your right leg in front of your left, so that your feet are crossed. Then jump back to the feet apart position, then do another jump so that your left foot crosses over your right and your feet are crossed again. Keep jumping in this way, to the beat, as you recite: "Cat's got the measles, dog's got the flu, chicken's got the chickenpox and so have you!" If your child wants to, you can make it into a game so that the one who ends up with her legs crossed is "out".

Get your child to see if she can pick up something small, such as a pencil or a piece of Lego, between her toes and put it in a box.

1 1 7

• Play "follow my leader" or "Simon says" - this helps your child learn to concentrate, to copy, to listen and follow instructions.

• Get your child to stand on your feet, facing you, and put her arms round you - then you start walking.

• Get your child to lie on her back and hug her knees. Then ask her to rock herself up into a sitting position without any help from you, and without using her hands. At first she'll roll over to the sides - but as she gets stronger she'll be able to sit up.

• Ask her to curl up into a very tight parcel, hugging her knees to her chest, face down on the floor. You pick her up around her waist and she has to see how long she can stay curled up without coming "undone". She will enjoy trying to resist the power of gravity.

• Once she has got the idea of keeping her body curled up, this is a fun way of doing a forward roll. She stands behind you while you sit on the floor with legs outstretched and apart. She leans over your shoulder and you help her over so that she does a forward roll, keeping her body curled and her head tucked in, landing on her shoulders, then rolling onto her back.

• Sit sideways and get your child to put her arms round your neck and her legs round your waist, then go forward onto all fours so she is underneath you. At first you might need to put one arm round her to support her. It's hard work, and she won't have the strength to cling on for long, but she will love being a "baby monkey"!

"On rainy days, when Adam needs to work off some surplus energy but we can't go out, I take all the cushions off the chairs and sofa and pile them up in the middle of the room. He has a wonderful time jumping, climbing and rolling all over them!"

SHELLEY

- Roll your child up in a blanket like a mummy - then take one end and pull, so she does a roly-poly out of the blanket. If there are two of you, let your child lie in the middle of the blanket while each of you takes two corners and then swing her to and fro in it like a hammock.

- Make a little den in your living room by rearranging the furniture and draping sheets over it. Let her explore all the different openings she can squeeze out of.

- Pull your sofa away from the wall and she can use the space behind it as a narrow passageway to squeeze through, or a hiding place, or she could sit or stand behind it and perform a puppet show using the back of the sofa as the stage.

A good game for outside is to hold your child around the chest, with her back against yours, and swing her round and round.

- A double bed is an irresistible place for a child who loves jumping and bouncing around.

    She might like this song:
"Three little monkeys, jumping on the bed
One fell off and bumped his head
Mummy phoned the doctor, the doctor said: 'No more monkeys jumping on the bed!'"

⚠ **Play safely**
Until the age of around three, it's best to hold your child around the chest when you swing her through the air. After three it should be safe to swing her by the arms or wrists. If you are swinging your child by the arms, hold her by both forearms. By holding just one you could strain her elbow. Holding her forearms is better than holding her by the hands - hands tend to be slippery and you could lose your grip.

Looking To The Future

Do we really need to think about whether our children are "fit"? Surely any normal child gets enough exercise to grow up healthy without parents having to make a conscious effort to ensure she is physically active?

Times have changed. In earlier generations, even quite young children played outside a lot, in the streets or in open spaces near their homes - running about, playing ball games, riding bikes, exploring the woods and fields, fishing in the canal. But most children today don't experience the joys of "playing out". Many of them spend much of their time indoors, because parents are afraid to let them out for fear of traffic and other dangers.

Cooped up within four walls, they discover the joys of television and videos, games machines and computers. If we aren't careful, today's children will become a generation of couch potatoes.

Children become less physically active as they grow. There is a decline in their level of physical activity from the age of five to 16. Unfit children all too often grow up into unfit adults. Research has shown that even young children sometimes show the early signs of risk factors associated with heart disease, such as high levels of cholesterol, too much body fat and too little physical activity. Experts believe that coronary heart disease in adult life has its origins in childhood.

Research on children's activity levels carried out at the Children's Health and Exercise Centre, School of Education, University of Exeter, has come up with some alarming findings. Professor Neil Armstrong and his colleagues studied junior and secondary schoolchildren, monitoring their heart rates during their normal activities, and concluded that young children are not nearly physically active enough.

Among secondary schoolchildren, over a third of the boys and over half of the girls did not have a single 10-minute period equivalent to brisk walking during three weekdays of monitoring.

If you have a lively three or four-year-old this probably seems irrelevant and you'd heave a sigh of relief if only she would sit down quietly for a few minutes. But it is worth thinking about.

Experts believe that if you are going to be a physically active person, this behaviour pattern is most likely to start in childhood and adolescence. In other words, active children tend to grow up to be active in adult life too. By encouraging your child to take physical exercise and to be active now, while she is young, you could be helping her chances of a healthy old age.

Heart disease is one risk that is reduced if you take regular exercise. Osteoporosis, the bone-thinning disease which particularly affects women in later life, also has its roots in early life. By taking regular weight-bearing exercise - like running, jogging, skipping, tennis - you can build up bone strength. But bone strength can only be built in the first 25 to 30 years of life.

Mothers are the main role models for young children. Most research studies which have looked at this have found that primary schoolchildren's physical activity has been significantly correlated with the activity levels of their parents. In other words, if you are an active person, your child is likely to be the same.

Girls And Boys Come Out To Play

If you have a daughter, it is even more important to encourage her to be physically active. Research shows that boys tend to be more active than girls, even in the first few years, and between the ages of six and 17 the difference between the sexes becomes more marked. When they reach the age of 11, the activity levels of girls often plummet.

Parents often treat their sons and daughters differently, without even realizing it. Research has shown that boys receive more support and encouragement from their parents to be physically active. Even very early on, boys are allowed more freedom to engage in vigorous activities whereas girls are encouraged to be more dependent and less exploratory. Parents with daughters, please take note!

The Great Outdoors

When children are outside they tend to be more physically active than when they are in the house. Unless you live in a mansion, it's only outdoors that your child can really run as fast as her legs will carry her, and carry on running until she is puffed out. By heading for a wide open space where it's safe to let go of her hand, you are giving her the freedom to find out how far and how fast she can go.

Here she also has the space to pedal and steer her tricycle and to learn to kick, to throw and to catch a ball without it ending up in the neighbour's garden. If she can develop her skills at this age - and find out that it's fun - it will give her the confidence and motivation to enjoy PE and sport later on.

Set her targets that you know she can reach - failure will discourage her and spoil her enjoyment. When she succeeds in doing something, that feeling of achievement is rewarding and makes her want to repeat the experience. Praise her for her efforts - your approval is a reward too.

Try to make a regular trip to the park or open space, maybe with her bike, her ball, a frisbee or a kite. As well as teaching her to kick the ball, let her have a try at being the goalie. Or pit your strength against hers - hold the ball tightly between your knees and see if she can manage to pull it out.

In The Garden

A garden gives lots of scope for play activities. Even if you haven't got a slide or swing, you can make your garden a fun place to be. You could make an obstacle course for your child to negotiate, with blankets to wriggle under, plant pots to weave around, boxes to jump over, a tunnel, tyre or big cardboard box to crawl through.

Fill a pillowcase with scrunched-up newspaper, tie it at the top and suspend it from a clothes line for her to use as a punchbag, or let her have a "kicking box", an old cardboard box that she can kick round the garden with no fear of it flying over the garden fence.

The garden is also a wonderful place for messy play, when the weather is good enough. Let your child loose with her paints and that cardboard box again, or let her make paint footprints by stepping in a tray of paint and walking all over a length of old wallpaper. Something else that children love is being allowed to "paint" the walls of the house with a big bucket of water and a grown-up paintbrush.

Your child will enjoy playing with water outside, and you don't need to worry about the floor getting soaked. If it's not warm enough for a paddling pool, let her sit in front of her old baby bath full of water and lots of containers and floating toys. This will keep her happily occupied for ages - but don't leave her alone, as children can drown even in a few inches of water.

Clubs And Classes

Some children enjoy doing activities in clubs and classes. As well as the social side - learning to be with other children, taking turns, listening to instructions and so on - a class can enrich your child's life by introducing her to something new, such as dance, swimming, judo or ice-skating. At the very least this gets you and your child out of the house and gives your child some physical activity. If you are really lucky your child will discover something she enjoys and is good at, which could form the basis of a lifelong hobby.

This kind of activity is also good for a child's self-esteem. She will get a sense of achievement from mastering a new challenge and improving her performance.

What's available will depend on where you live, of course. In a city you may have quite a few different activities to choose from, but in a small town or village there probably won't be as much on offer.

Weigh up the relative merits of the different activities. Think about what your child is likely to enjoy, but also consider the cost of the class and all the other things you might eventually have to buy, such as ballet shoes and leotard. Consider how convenient it will be to get to the class. How long will it take you to get there and back? And can you really bear to get up at 7.30 every Saturday morning for a 9 a.m. swimming class? You need a lie-in too!

Look for a good ratio of adults to children - this means closer supervision and less waiting around for their turn. And make sure the facilities are good - for your child and for you. No matter how much she likes the class, it takes the gloss off if you have to spend an hour waiting in a pokey room on a hard chair, or if she has to change in a cold corridor.

Ask if your child can try it out a few times to make sure she likes it before you spend money on a whole term's classes or kitting her out with the right clothes.

To find a class, ask at your local leisure centre, library or swimming pool, or ring the local council's leisure services department. Ask around among your friends, especially those with older children. Or contact the national organizations listed overleaf, who should be able to tell you about local classes.

Many activities are open to children of a surprisingly young age. Children can start ice-skating at around four - though some exceptional children ice-skate as young as two. Some riding schools take children of four. And even some karate and judo classes take under-fives.

Swimming lessons, where your child goes into the water with a teacher rather than with you, start at three or four years old depending on the policy of the swimming pool. If your child isn't very brave in the water with you or won't try to swim, a teacher might have more success.

Tumble Tots is a physical play programme with sessions for children of different age groups, with some classes starting as early as six months. From the age of around three you leave your child at the class rather than joining in with her. As well as ladders, tunnels, ropes and trestles to be tackled, there are songs and activities to teach the children about numbers, shapes and colours. To find your nearest class, contact Tumble Tots (details over the page).

Pre-school gym classes, for children from around three, are also available in some leisure centres. There are around 1000 gym clubs nationwide that are approved by the British Amateur Gymnastics Association - phone the BAGA to find your nearest club.

For some useful addresses and phone numbers, see over the page.

Useful Addresses

Amateur Swimming Association, Harold Fern House, Derby Square, Loughborough, LE11 5AL, tel: 01509 230431.

British Amateur Gymnastics Association, Ford Hall, Lilleshall National Sports Centre, Nr Newport, Shropshire TF10 9NB, tel: 01952 820330.

Child Accident Prevention Trust, 4th Floor, 18-20 Farringdon Lane, London EC1R 3AU, tel: 0171-608 3828.

National Association of Toy and Leisure Libraries, 68 Churchway, London NW1 1LT, tel: 0171-387 9592.

National Childbirth Trust, Alexandra House, Oldham Terrace, Acton, London W3 6NH, tel: 0181-992 8637.

Pre-School Learning Alliance, 69 Kings Cross Road, London WC1X 9LL, tel: 0171-833 0991.

Tumble Tots UK Ltd, Blue Bird Park, Bromsgrove Road, Hunnington, Halesowen, West Midlands, B62 OEN, tel: 0121-585 7003.

Acknowledgements

Thanks to M.O.T. for such great models:
Maya and Cheyanne
Caroline and Ivan
Theresa and Georgina
Marc and Jedd
Felicity and Milo
Sofie and Lily

Picture Credits
All special photography by J. Catt
Courtesy of Tumble Tots 127
Science Photo Library:
Alex Bartel 11
Oscar Burriel 12
Lupe Cunha: 13, 14, 22, 70, 85, 101, 102, 126

Fisher-Price